The Collins-Longman Atlas Programme

MAPSTART 3

Simon Catling

Senior Lecturer in Primary Curricula, Oxford Polytechnic

Contents

Looking down

Block of flats, numbers 1–31

Terraced house, number 22

Detached house, number 1A

A is an **oblique aerial photo.**
In the centre you can see a block of flats. The area around the flats is called Hillmead. It is in the north of the town of Norwich. Hillmead is a residential area. The roads are lined by people's homes. Photos **B**, **C** and **D** show three types of home in Hillmead.

E is a **vertical aerial photo** of the same area. **H** is a **map** of Hillmead. Use the **key** to see what the shapes and colours mean.
On the map and aerial photos find where the homes in photos **B**, **C** and **D** are in Hillmead.

1 Which is the tallest building in Hillmead?
2 What are the numbers of the homes on each side of the home in photo **C**?
3 Find the home in photo **D** on map **H**. From the map, draw its shape.
4 How many rows of terraced houses are there in Hillmead?
5 Use the photos and map to work out how many flats are in the block of flats in photo **B**.
6 Which home in Hillmead is furthest from number 14?

7 The building in photo **F** is not in Hillmead. Say which roads go past it.
8 Imagine you walked from flat 9 to house number 114. Describe which way you would go and what you would pass.
9 Look at photo **G**. Use photos **A** and **E** and map **H** to work out what it shows. From in front of which home was the photo taken?
10 Find Norwich on the map on page 28. Say which country it is in.

F

G

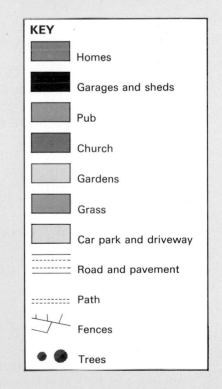

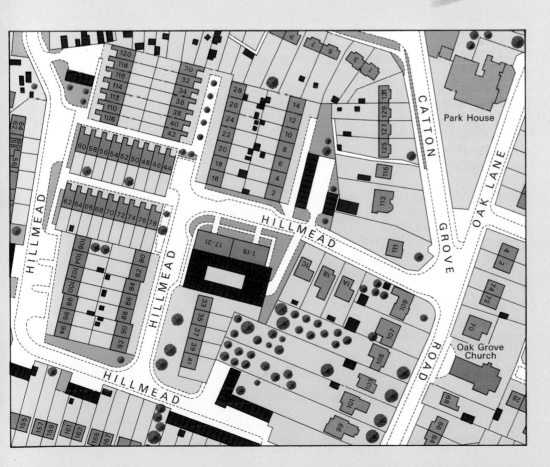

KEY

	Homes
	Garages and sheds
	Pub
	Church
	Gardens
	Grass
	Car park and driveway
- - -	Road and pavement
----	Path
	Fences
● ●	Trees

Grid references

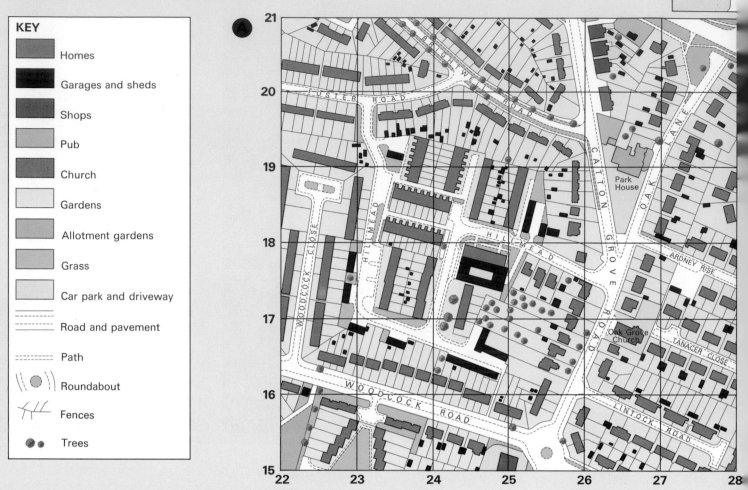

KEY

	Homes
	Garages and sheds
	Shops
	Pub
	Church
	Gardens
	Allotment gardens
	Grass
	Car park and driveway
	Road and pavement
	Path
	Roundabout
	Fences
	Trees

Map **A** shows the area around Hillmead. It is in the centre of the map. The size of everything on the map has been reduced.

Grid lines have been drawn over the map. Each line has been given a number. The **black** numbers increase from left to right along the bottom of the map. They name the vertical lines. The **red** numbers increase from bottom to top along the side of the map. They name the horizontal lines. These numbers help us name the **grid squares.**

Look at drawing **B** and follow the instructions below to find the block of flats in grid square **24, 17** on the map.

- Put one finger on the black number **24** at the bottom of map **A**.
- Put another finger on the red number **17** at the side of map **A**.
- Move both fingers along the grid lines until they meet.
- Where the two lines cross is the lower left corner of the grid square **24,17**

You have used the **four-figure grid reference** to find the block of flats in Hillmead.

? Name three features in each grid square:
   1 **22,16**   2 **26,19**   3 **25,18**

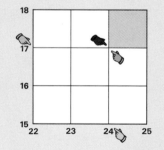

How to find a grid square.

Now find the church. To tell someone its grid reference you must:

- Put your fingers on the grid lines at the lower left corner of the grid square the church is in.
- Follow the vertical and horizontal lines to the edge of the map.
- Write the number of the vertical line first, then the number of the horizontal line.

? 4 What is the church's grid reference?
  5 Give the grid reference for the roundabout.
  6 Give the grid reference for the shops nearest the pub.

Compass directions

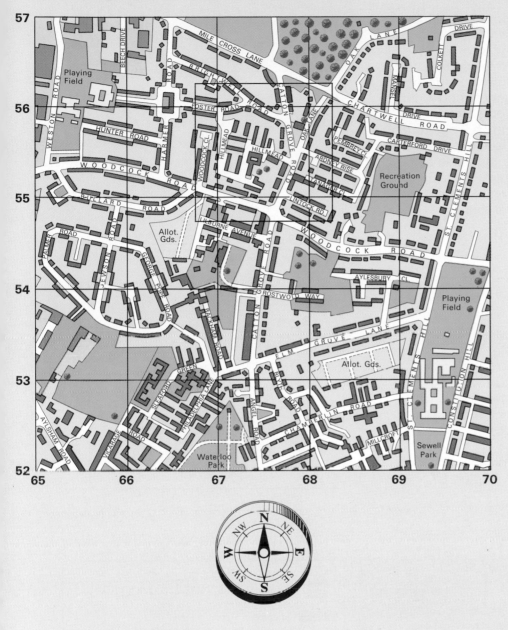

KEY

�e	Buildings
▪	Shops
☐	School
▪	Church
▪	Factory
☐	Gardens
▪	Park and grass
☐	Open ground
—	Road
- - -	Path
● ●	Trees
Allot. Gds.	Allotment gardens
CL.	Close
RD.	Road

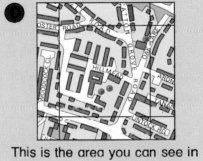

This is the area you can see in map **A**. Find it in map **C**.

Map **C** shows more of the area around Hillmead. Everything has been reduced further in size to fit in more of the area.

The shapes and colours show what the features on the map are. Use the key to check what these symbols mean.

Hillmead is at grid reference **67,55**. It is in the north of the map. Look at the area north of Hillmead, and find Foster Road and Brightwell Road. These roads are north of Hillmead. North is a **compass direction**. Compass directions help us to say in which direction places are. The first road south of Hillmead is Woodcock Road.

? 1 Which road goes along the east side of Hillmead?
2 Go south along Catton Grove Road to Elm Grove Lane. Is Elm Grove Lane east or west of Catton Grove Road?
3 Name another road that goes north-south.
4 Which direction is Hillmead from the junction of Woodcock Road and Catton Grove Road?

? 5 What are the buildings on the southwest of the junction of Woodcock Road and Catton Grove Road in grid square **67,54** used for?
6 Which direction is Hillmead from the school in grid square **69,52**?
7 Name the roads you would pass on the north side, if you turned east into Woodcock Road from Weston Road and walked along to the recreation ground.

Measuring the map

A is a vertical photo of a bench. You can see the whole bench because the photo shows it smaller than it really is. Photo **B** shows it reduced to an even smaller size. Plan **C** shows the bench the same size as it is in photo **B**. Plan **C** has been drawn accurately, so that it can be used to find out the length and width of the real bench. One centimetre (cm) on the plan measures one metre (m) of the real bench. This is the **scale** of the plan. The **scale bar** is used to measure distances on the plan. You can use the scale bar between **C** and **D** to measure the plans in them. **E** is a plan of a classroom. It has been drawn to scale. 1cm on the plan measures 1m of the real room.

?

1 How long are these:
  a the bench in plan **C**?
  b the table in plan **D**?
  c the classroom in plan **E**?
2 Which objects in plan **D** are longer than 1m?
3 How long is the longest object in plan **D**?
4 Name three objects in the classroom which are less than 1m long.
5 How far is it in a straight line from the left hand sink to the window opposite, in plan **E**?

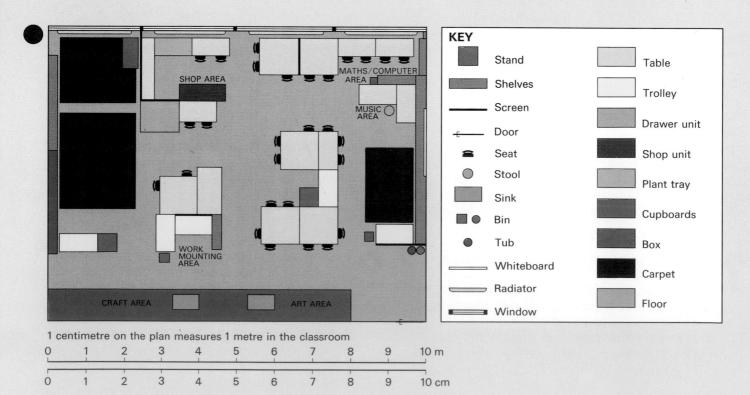

A

B

C ▬ Bench

1 centimetre on the plan measures 1 metre on the object

| 0 | 1 | 2 | 3 | 4 m |
| 0 | 1 | 2 | 3 | 4 cm |

D
☐ Table
⟜ Bicycle
◁▷ Boat
🚗 Car

1 centimetre on the plan measures 1 metre in the classroom

| 0 | 1 | 2 | 3 | 4 | 5 | 6 | 7 | 8 | 9 | 10 m |
| 0 | 1 | 2 | 3 | 4 | 5 | 6 | 7 | 8 | 9 | 10 cm |

SHOP AREA
MATHS/COMPUTER AREA
MUSIC AREA
WORK MOUNTING AREA
CRAFT AREA
ART AREA

KEY

Stand	Table
Shelves	Trolley
Screen	Drawer unit
Door	Shop unit
Seat	Plant tray
Stool	Cupboards
Sink	Box
Bin	Carpet
Tub	Floor
Whiteboard	
Radiator	
Window	

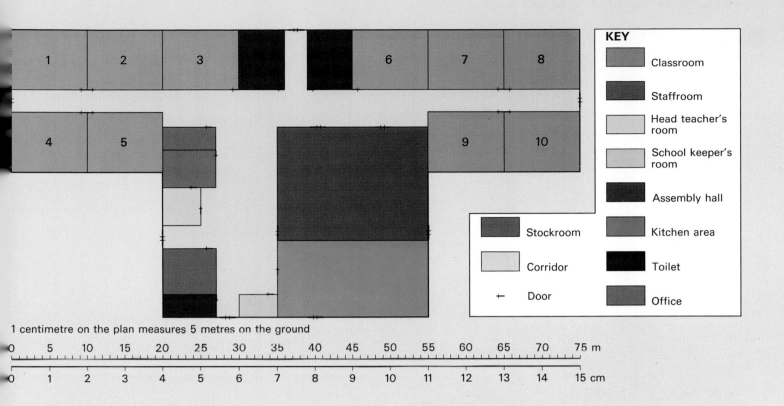

KEY

- Classroom
- Staffroom
- Head teacher's room
- School keeper's room
- Assembly hall
- Stockroom
- Kitchen area
- Corridor
- Toilet
- ← Door
- Office

1 centimetre on the plan measures 5 metres on the ground

| 0 | 5 | 10 | 15 | 20 | 25 | 30 | 35 | 40 | 45 | 50 | 55 | 60 | 65 | 70 | 75 m |

| 0 | 1 | 2 | 3 | 4 | 5 | 6 | 7 | 8 | 9 | 10 | 11 | 12 | 13 | 14 | 15 cm |

To show the whole of the school building on this page, its plan has to be drawn to a smaller scale. **F** is a plan of the school building. The scale bar shows that 1 cm on the plan measures 5 m of the real school building. In plan **G** the school building is drawn to an even smaller scale. Plan **G** shows all the school grounds. 1 cm on plan **G** measures 10 m of the real school grounds. Plans **E**, **F** and **G** show that the more area you want to show on a plan, the smaller the scale must become.

?

1 Which plan shows the most area of ground?
2 How long is the school building from east to west?
3 Measure how far it is along the corridor from the door of classroom 3 to the door of classroom 8 in plan **F**.
4 In plan **G**, how far is it from the school entrance along the path to the playground?

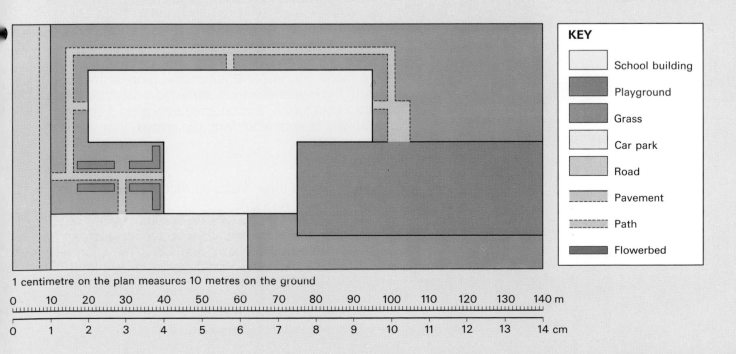

KEY

- School building
- Playground
- Grass
- Car park
- Road
- Pavement
- Path
- Flowerbed

1 centimetre on the plan measures 10 metres on the ground

| 0 | 10 | 20 | 30 | 40 | 50 | 60 | 70 | 80 | 90 | 100 | 110 | 120 | 130 | 140 m |

| 0 | 1 | 2 | 3 | 4 | 5 | 6 | 7 | 8 | 9 | 10 | 11 | 12 | 13 | 14 cm |

Maps as records

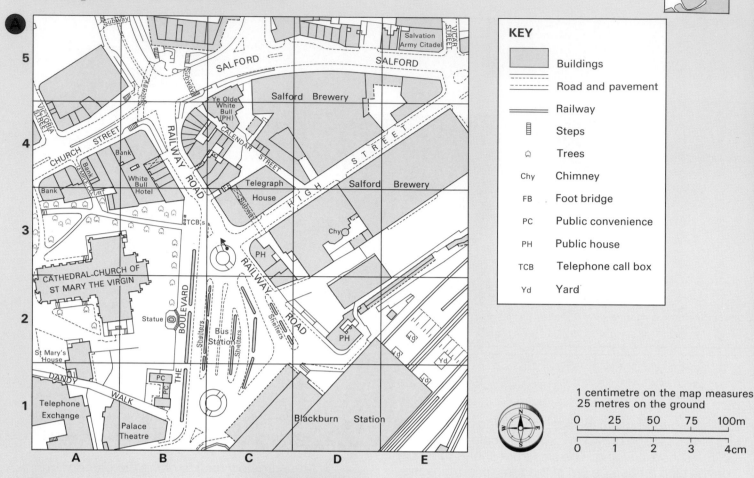

KEY

▨	Buildings
- - -	Road and pavement
═══	Railway
▤	Steps
⌂	Trees
Chy	Chimney
FB	Foot bridge
PC	Public convenience
PH	Public house
TCB	Telephone call box
Yd	Yard

1 centimetre on the map measures
25 metres on the ground

```
0    25    50    75    100m
|----|----|----|----|
0    1     2     3     4cm
```

Map **A** shows the area around Railway Road in the town of Blackburn. Photo **B** shows what Railway Road looks like. The arrow in grid square **C3** shows where photo **B** was taken from, looking northwest. Map **A** and photo **B** show how Railway Road looks now. Photo **C** shows how Railway Road looked in 1907. See how many changes you can spot. Map **D** is even older. It shows Railway Road in 1893. By looking at maps **D** and **A** you can see what changes have taken place in the area. This is because the maps are records of how the area looks at the time the maps are made. **E** is another map of the same area, but it was drawn to show how the area might look in the future. It is an imaginary map. Look at it carefully to spot what features remain that you can see in map **A**.

?
1 Name three features that are the same in maps **A** and **E**.
2 Which feature in map **D** remains in map **E**?
3 In which direction are you looking along Railway Road in photo **C**?
4 Use the scale bar to measure how long Railway Road is in map **A**. Is High Street longer?
5 Find Blackburn on the map on pages 24 and 25. Which country is it in?

8

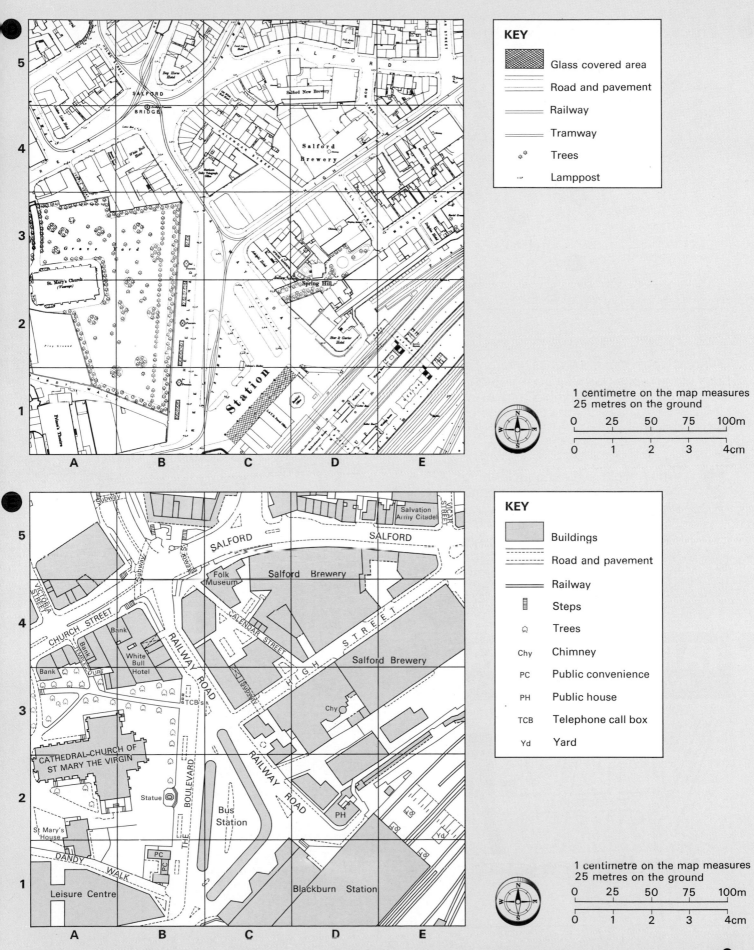

KEY

▨	Glass covered area
	Road and pavement
	Railway
	Tramway
♣	Trees
⌐	Lamppost

1 centimetre on the map measures
25 metres on the ground

0   25   50   75   100m

0   1   2   3   4cm

KEY

▨	Buildings
	Road and pavement
	Railway
▤	Steps
⌂	Trees
Chy	Chimney
PC	Public convenience
PH	Public house
TCB	Telephone call box
Yd	Yard

1 centimetre on the map measures
25 metres on the ground

0   25   50   75   100m

0   1   2   3   4cm

Maps around us

A

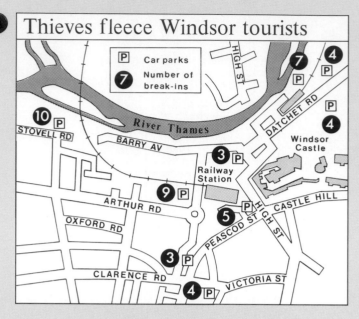

Thieves fleece Windsor tourists

P — Car parks
7 — Number of break-ins

Different types of maps give us different information. Look at the maps on these pages. Each map has a different purpose. For example, map **A** comes from a newspaper; it shows the car parks where there have been break-ins.

?
1 When might someone look at map **E**?
2 Why would someone use map **B**?
3 Why would a shop put a map in an advert?
4 The postcard map has no key. Make a key to show what the symbols on the map mean.
5 Make a collection of everyday maps like these. See what other maps you can add to your collection.

B

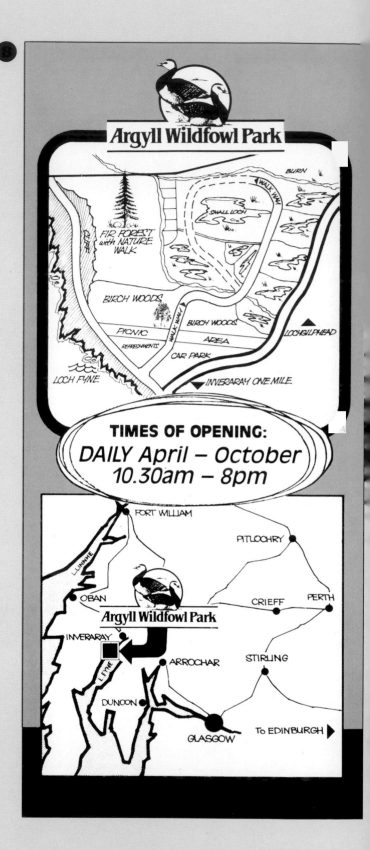

Argyll Wildfowl Park

TIMES OF OPENING:
DAILY April – October
10.30am – 8pm

C

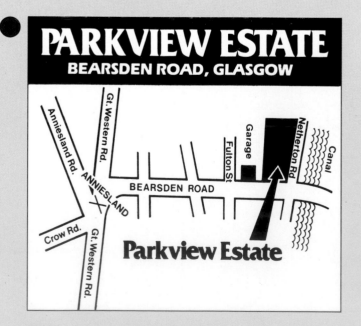

PARKVIEW ESTATE
BEARSDEN ROAD, GLASGOW

Landshape – hills on maps

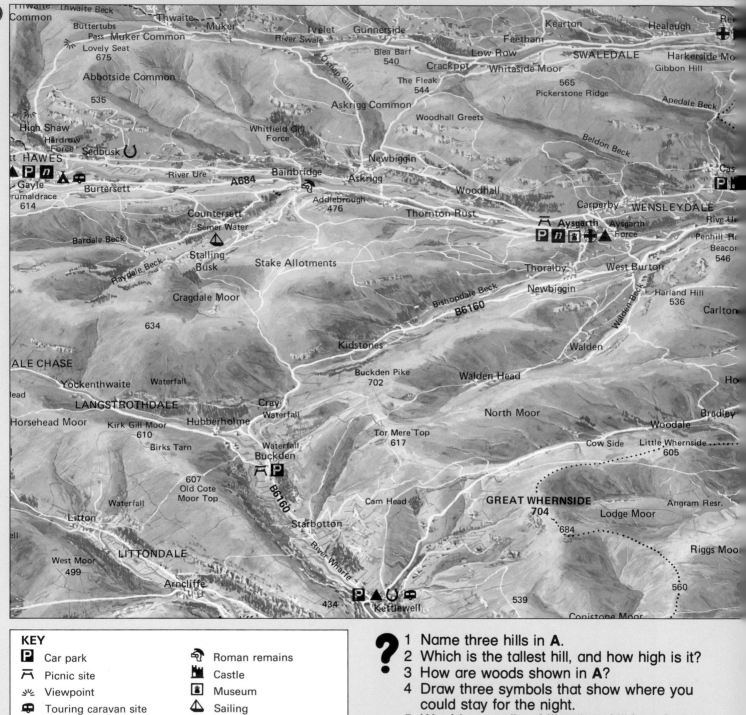

KEY

P	Car park		Roman remains
	Picnic site		Castle
	Viewpoint		Museum
	Touring caravan site		Sailing
	Camping site	U	Horse riding / Trekking
▲	Youth hostel	**n**	National park centre
	Mountain rescue post	.....	National park boundary
---	Pennine Way	546	Heights in metres

A is an oblique aerial view of part of Yorkshire Dales National Park. In the picture you can see roads, lakes, rivers, villages and many hills. This oblique view also shows places where you can park, camp and visit. Many of the hills are high and steep sided. The number next to the name of each hill tells you how high it is in metres.

?

1 Name three hills in **A**.
2 Which is the tallest hill, and how high is it?
3 How are woods shown in **A**?
4 Draw three symbols that show where you could stay for the night.
5 Would you walk uphill or downhill from Semer Water to the top of Cragdale Moor?
6 You are driven from Kettlewell to Aysgarth in a car. Write about what you would go past, and where you would go up and down hill.
7 Find Yorkshire Dales National Park on the map of the British Isles on page 31. Is it in northern or southern England?

B is an old map. It was made by a famous mapmaker named John Speed in 1610. It shows most of the area that you can see in A. On his map, Speed showed the villages and rivers. The rivers are shown by lines and the towns by the symbol of a church. He also showed the land was hilly by drawing hill shapes as symbols on the map. These **hillocks** show where hills are. Find Penhill Beacon on A and B. Look for other places that are shown on both maps. For some you will find the spelling has changed.

Later mapmakers, like Christopher Greenwood, tried to show a clearer picture of the shape of the land by using symbols called **hachures**, which are short, thin lines drawn close together. Map C, printed in 1817, also shows part of the same area as B. On it hachures are used to show which way and how much the land slopes. The hachures always point downhill. From the hachures you can see where some land is higher or lower than other land.

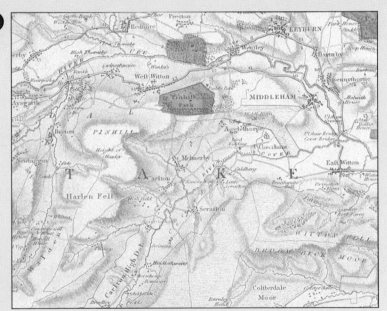

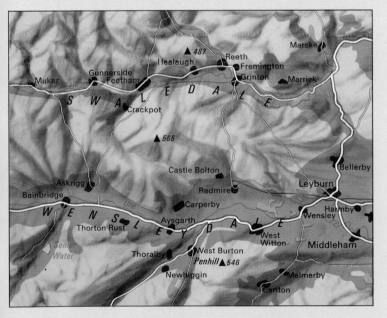

Present day mapmakers want to show this too. Map D shows one way this is done. **Hill-shading** is used to show the shape and slope of the land. Some of the hilltops are shown by a symbol, a name and the height in metres.

? 1 How are rivers shown on map C?
2 Which of maps B, C and D is the oldest?
3 How is map B similar to A?
4 Name three features that appear on each map.
5 Which map do you think shows the hills best?
6 Maps B and C do not have a key, make one for each map.

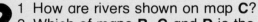

KEY

Moorland		Farmland		Main road
Forest and woodland		Town		Secondary road
▲487 Spot height in metres		Railway		Other road

Landshape – contours

Photo labels: Neuadd Wen, Road, Pen-y-graig, Church, Hotel, Cartref, Gray Stones

Map labels include: Pen-llain, Clegyr-bâch, Gwenithnant, Pen-y-foel, Llys Myfyr, Gray Stones, Nant-y-dwr, Spr, Tegfan, Voel Vanna, Cartref, Hillside, Maen-y-fantell, Tyddyn-y-don, Ysgubor-bâch, Cave Path, Ch, GP, Pen-y-graig, Hotel, Pant-yr-eglwys, Neuadd Wen, Gadlys, Merddyn-fadyn, Glan-yr-afon, Swtan, Ty Newydd, GP, Caerau

141m, 105m, 85m, 75m, 57m, 50m, 35m, 25m, 22m, 28m, 32m, 65m

KEY

Symbol	Feature	Symbol	Feature
Road	Road	Building	Building
Track	Track	Public building	Public building
Field boundaries	Field boundaries	Ch	Church
Scrub	Scrub	GP	Guide post
Heath	Heath	Spr	Spring
Rock outcrop	Rock outcrop	W	Well

Contours are at 5 metres vertical interval

·163m Heights in metres

Direction of flow of water — Stream

Water (Sea)

Photo **A** shows a landscape in Anglesey, an island off the north west coast of Wales. You can see the same area in map **B**. The red cross on the map marks the place where photo **A** was taken. **A** looks north towards a church and a hill. Find the church on map **B**. The hill lies north of it. The hilltop is marked on map **B** by a dot, called a **spot height**. The spot height has a number next to it, 141m, which shows how high, in metres, the land is above sea level at that place. The hill has a round **shape**. Its shape and **slope** are shown on map **B** by thin brown lines called **contour lines**. A number shows how **high**, in metres, the land is above sea level along each contour line. From the contour lines we can see **which way** the land slopes and **how much** it slopes. Contour lines close together mean a steep slope. Where they are far apart the slope is gentle.

? Use map **B**. (Photo **A** will help you too.)
1. Find the spot height 65m. Does it mark a hilltop?
2. Find another spot height. Write its height.
3. Find the church and the hotel. Is the church on higher or lower ground than the hotel?
4. Is the slope north of the church gentle or steep?
5. You walk from the guide post near the church to Gray Stones house along the road. Do you go up or down hill? Say what you pass.

Landshape – the Pathfinder map

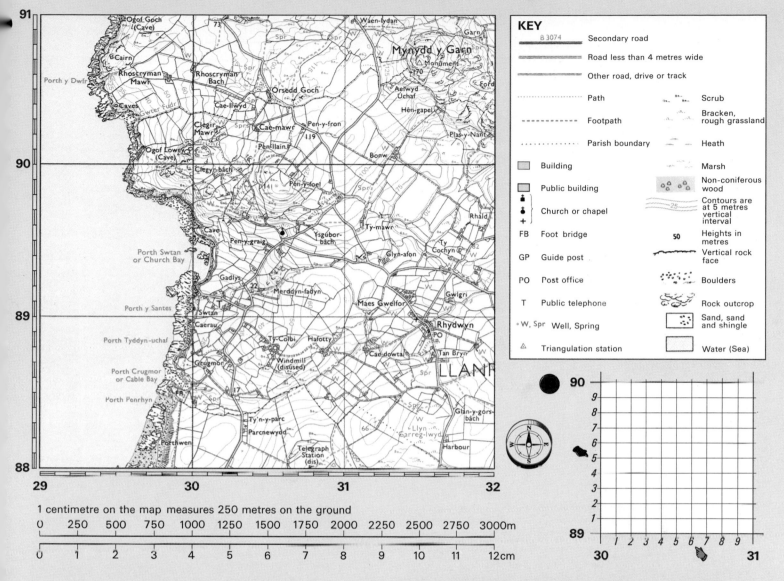

1 centimetre on the map measures 250 metres on the ground

Map **C** shows more of the landscape of Anglesey around the area you can see in photo **A** and map **B**. The church you can see in photo **A** is in grid square **30,89**. To say exactly where it is, it helps to give a grid reference that shows its site **inside** the grid square. To do this, we must imagine the grid square has been divided into one hundred smaller squares, like diagram **D**. We can then give the church a **six-figure grid reference** by counting the tenths along the southern and western sides of the square. The church is on the sixth line east of grid line **30**, and on the fifth line north of grid line **89**. Its six-figure grid reference is **306,895**. Photo **A** was taken at grid reference **304,889**. Find this spot on map **C**. The contour lines on map **C** show how hilly the landscape is. Look carefully and you will see the shape of several hills. Spot heights mark the top of some, such as spot height 141 at grid reference **305,898**

? Use map **C**.

1 Give the six-figure grid references of another spot height.
2 Is there a hilltop at **314,897** or at **312,883**?
3 You are walking northwest along the footpath at **317,903**. Do you go uphill or downhill?
4 Look at the coastline. Does the land slope steeply or gently to the sea?

? 5 You live at Caerau **302,889**, and go by car to the post office at Rhydwyn **315,889**
   a In which direction is the post office from home?
   b Do you go uphill or downhill from home to the post office?
   c How far is the post office from home in a straight line and by road?
   d If you walked to the post office instead, describe your route along footpaths.

Changing scale – neighbourhoods and towns

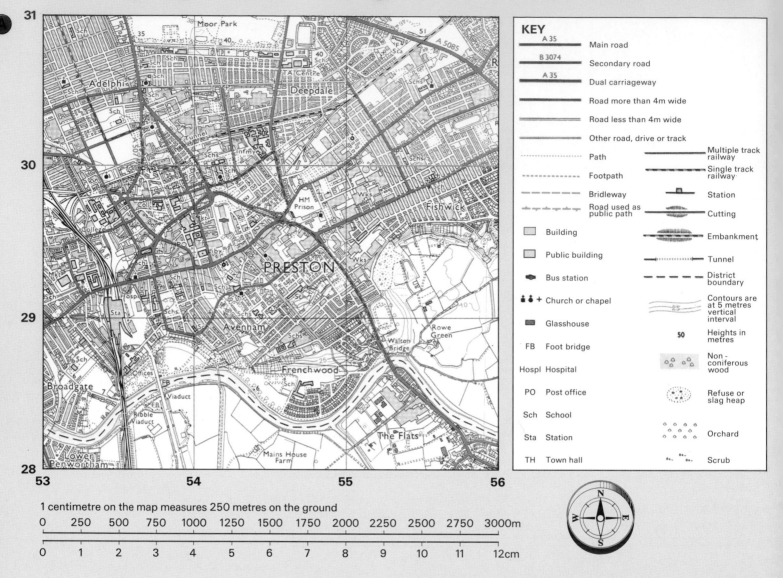

KEY

A 35	Main road
B 3074	Secondary road
A 35	Dual carriageway
	Road more than 4m wide
	Road less than 4m wide
	Other road, drive or track
Path	Multiple track railway
Footpath	Single track railway
Bridleway	Station
Road used as public path	Cutting

Building
Public building
Bus station
Church or chapel
Glasshouse
FB Foot bridge
Hospl Hospital
PO Post office
Sch School
Sta Station
TH Town hall

Embankment
Tunnel
District boundary
Contours are at 5 metres vertical interval
Heights in metres
Non-coniferous wood
Refuse or slag heap
Orchard
Scrub

1 centimetre on the map measures 250 metres on the ground

0 250 500 750 1000 1250 1500 1750 2000 2250 2500 2750 3000m

0   1   2   3   4   5   6   7   8   9   10   11   12cm

Map **A** shows part of the town of Preston in northwest England. Find the railway station. It is at grid reference **535,290**. You can see the shape of the station building.
In map **B** you can find the station at the same grid reference, but it is shown as a red circle. This is the symbol for a station. On this map the scale has been reduced to show more of Preston.
Map **C** is drawn at an even smaller scale to show all of Preston. Find the station in Preston.

1 Which symbol shows the station in map **C**?
2 Which of these maps would it be best to use to find the way if you were walking around the area near Preston Station? Say why.
3 Name two features which are shown on maps **A** and **B** by the same symbols.
4 How are buildings shown on each map?
5 Find the bridge at **537,285** in map **A**. Name three things you could probably see from it, looking west.

6 Look at map **B**. Imagine you were standing at **545,275** looking north. Would you be looking across fields or buildings to the river? What feature are you next to?
7 Use map **A**. If you walked from the chapel at **558,282** to the prison at **547,298** along the road:
   a in which direction would you walk?
   b how far would you walk?
   c what would you pass on your walk?
   d where would you have a steep walk uphill?

16

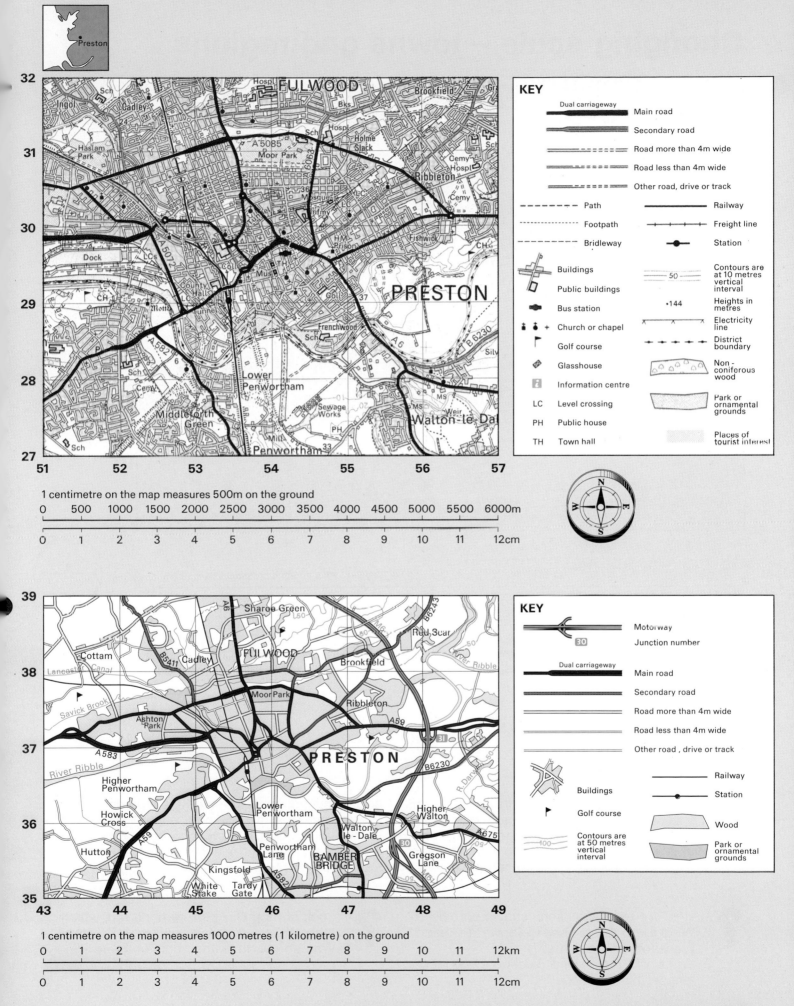

KEY

Dual carriageway	Main road
	Secondary road
	Road more than 4m wide
	Road less than 4m wide
	Other road, drive or track

Path		Railway
Footpath		Freight line
Bridleway		Station
Buildings		Contours are at 10 metres vertical interval
Public buildings	•144	Heights in metres
Bus station		Electricity line
Church or chapel		District boundary
Golf course		Non-coniferous wood
Glasshouse		Park or ornamental grounds
Information centre		Places of tourist interest
LC Level crossing		
PH Public house		
TH Town hall		

1 centimetre on the map measures 500m on the ground

0 500 1000 1500 2000 2500 3000 3500 4000 4500 5000 5500 6000m

0 1 2 3 4 5 6 7 8 9 10 11 12cm

KEY

	Motorway
30	Junction number
Dual carriageway	Main road
	Secondary road
	Road more than 4m wide
	Road less than 4m wide
	Other road, drive or track

Buildings		Railway
Golf course		Station
Contours are at 50 metres vertical interval		Wood
		Park or ornamental grounds

1 centimetre on the map measures 1000 metres (1 kilometre) on the ground

0 1 2 3 4 5 6 7 8 9 10 11 12km

0 1 2 3 4 5 6 7 8 9 10 11 12cm

Changing scale – towns and regions

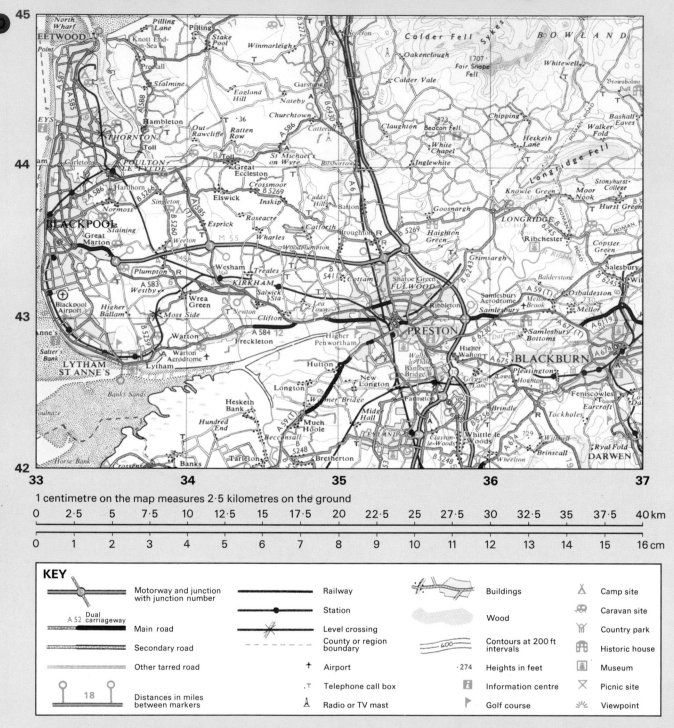

1 centimetre on the map measures 2·5 kilometres on the ground

| 0 | 2·5 | 5 | 7·5 | 10 | 12·5 | 15 | 17·5 | 20 | 22·5 | 25 | 27·5 | 30 | 32·5 | 35 | 37·5 | 40 km |

| 0 | 1 | 2 | 3 | 4 | 5 | 6 | 7 | 8 | 9 | 10 | 11 | 12 | 13 | 14 | 15 | 16 cm |

KEY

Symbol	Description	Symbol	Description	Symbol	Description	Symbol	Description
	Motorway and junction with junction number		Railway		Buildings	⚑	Camp site
A 52	Dual carriageway		Station		Wood		Caravan site
	Main road		Level crossing		Contours at 200 ft intervals		Country park
	Secondary road		County or region boundary	400			Historic house
	Other tarred road	✈	Airport	·274	Heights in feet		Museum
18	Distances in miles between markers	·T	Telephone call box	i	Information centre	✕	Picnic site
		⋏	Radio or TV mast	▶	Golf course		Viewpoint

Map **D** is drawn at a smaller scale than map **C** on page 17. It covers more of the area around Preston. On the west of the map you can see the seaside town of Blackpool. Look at the shape and size of both towns. Maps **E** and **F** are drawn at much smaller scales, but you can still see the shape and size of Preston and Blackpool on both maps. Map **D** shows all the main roads and many of the minor roads in the area, but on the small scale maps **E** and **F** only the most important roads are shown.

?
1 How are railway stations shown on map **D**?
2 What symbols are used to show Preston and Blackpool on each map?
3 Which of Preston and Blackpool has the longer, thinner shape?

?
4 Look at map **D**. Apart from the M6, which other main road goes north from Preston?
5 Why do you think that most of the roads on map **D** are not shown on map **F**?

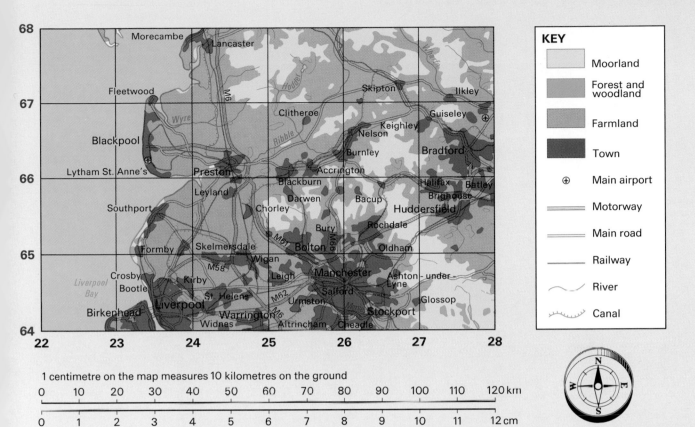

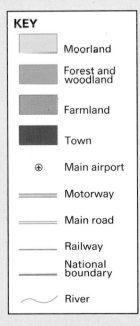

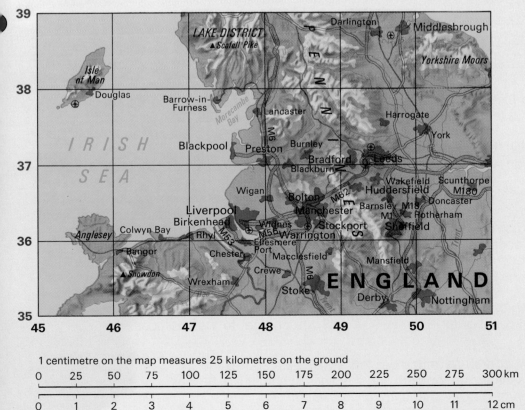

Introducing atlas maps

The title names the map.

The compass is used to work out directions on the map.

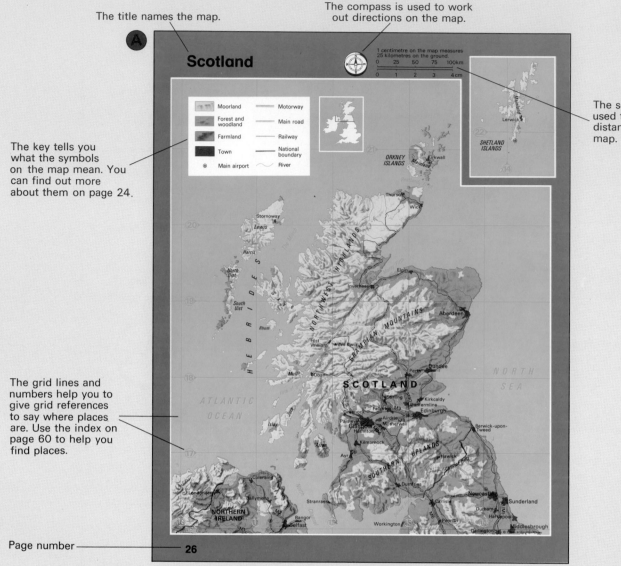

Scotland

1 centimetre on the map measures 25 kilometres on the ground.
0   25   50   75   100km
0   1   2   3   4cm

The scale bar is used to measure distances on the map.

The key tells you what the symbols on the map mean. You can find out more about them on page 24.

Moorland — Motorway
Forest and woodland — Main road
Farmland — Railway
Town — National boundary
⊕ Main airport — River

The grid lines and numbers help you to give grid references to say where places are. Use the index on page 60 to help you find places.

The maps you will explore in the following pages show the British Isles, Europe and the rest of the world.

A and **B** show two pages that have been reduced. The notes around **A** and **B** tell you what to use to understand the maps.

? Look at maps **A** and **B**.
1 What is the title of each map?
2 Are the maps drawn with south at the top or bottom of the map?
3 What are the grid references for Sunderland and Aswan?
4 Draw how a river is shown on each map.
5 What would you use the scale bar for?

Some of the maps are drawn like maps **A** and **B** to show how the land is used. They are called **environment maps**. You can find out more about them on pages 24 and 49.

Environment maps are one type of **thematic map**. **C** is part of a thematic map from page 35, which shows the position and shape of the countries in Europe. Thematic maps are drawn to show information about a special topic or theme. This is done to make it easier for you to find out about that topic from the map. Some maps show information about more than one theme, like map **D**. **D**, part of the map on page 28, shows the main towns in the British Isles. It also shows the main roads and railways so you can find out how you can get to these places.

It is important to remember that every map shows only selected information about a place, whether it is a map of a town, a country or the world.

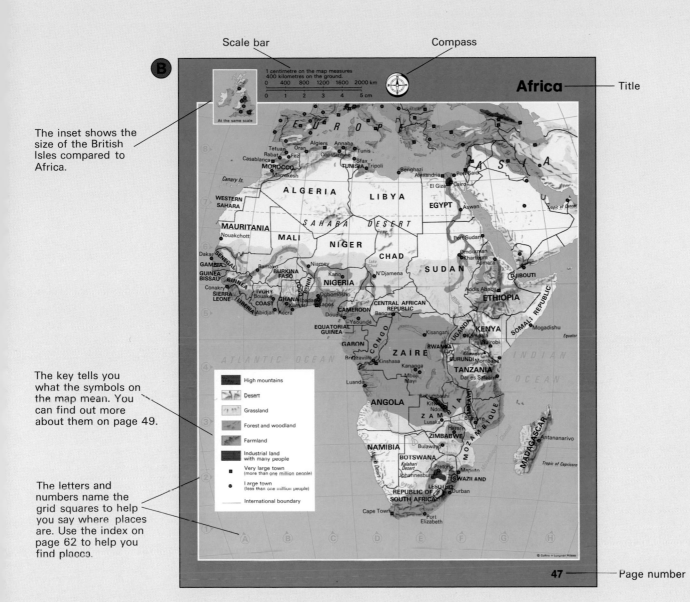

Scale bar

Compass

1 centimetre on the map measures 400 kilometres on the ground.

Africa

Title

The inset shows the size of the British Isles compared to Africa.

The key tells you what the symbols on the map mean. You can find out more about them on page 49.

The letters and numbers name the grid squares to help you say where places are. Use the index on page 62 to help you find places.

Key:
- High mountains
- Desert
- Grassland
- Forest and woodland
- Farmland
- Industrial land with many people
- ■ Very large town (more than one million people)
- ● Large town (less than one million people)
- — International boundary

47 — Page number

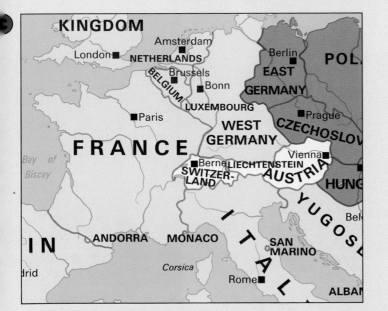

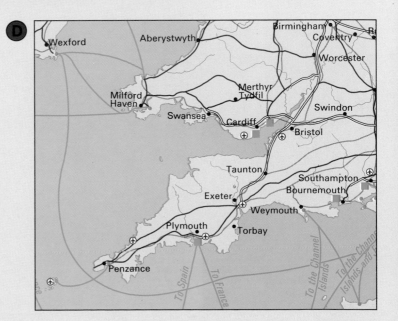

British Isles from Space

Above is a satellite photo of the British Isles. You can see the land and the sea. The map you can see opposite shows the same area. It tells us more about the land than the photo does. It shows the main types of environment such as farmland, moorland, towns and cities.

The large islands of Ireland and Britain are obvious on both the photo and the map. Use the map to help you find where the Shetland and Orkney islands, and the Isle of Man are on the photo. See which other islands you can find on both the photo and the map.

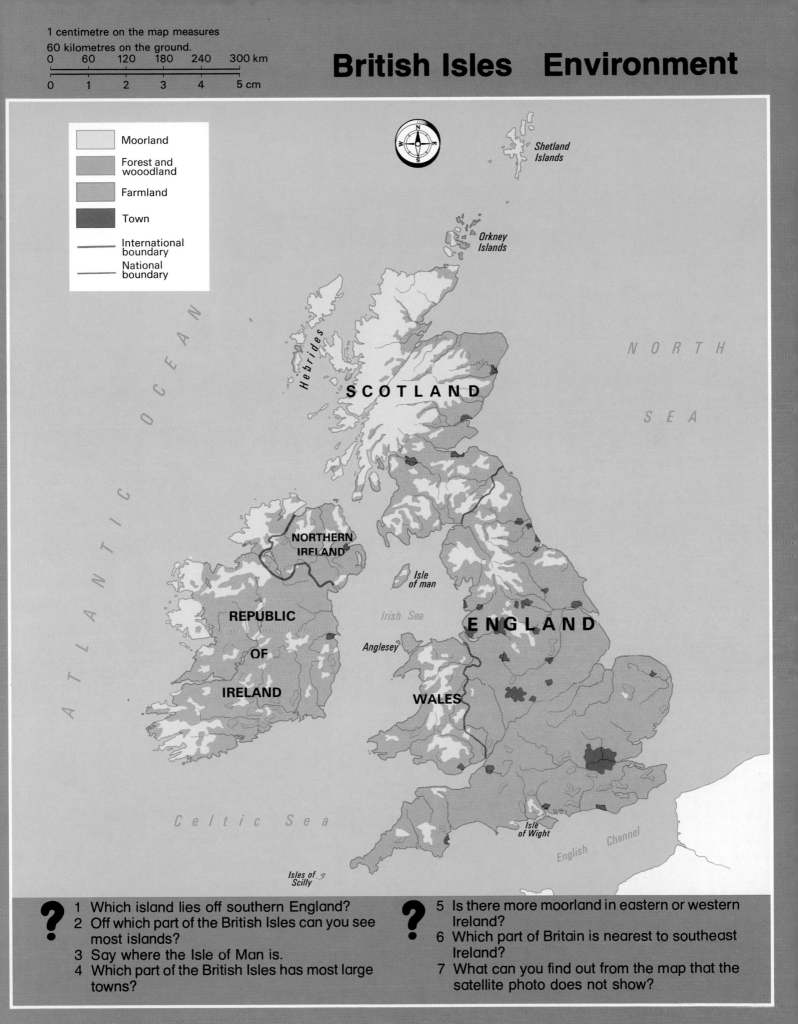

British Isles Environment

1 centimetre on the map measures
60 kilometres on the ground.

0	60	120	180	240	300 km
0	1	2	3	4	5 cm

Legend:
- Moorland
- Forest and wooodland
- Farmland
- Town
- International boundary
- National boundary

NORTH SEA

Shetland Islands

Orkney Islands

Hebrides

SCOTLAND

ATLANTIC OCEAN

NORTHERN IRELAND

REPUBLIC OF IRELAND

Isle of man

Irish Sea

ENGLAND

Anglesey

WALES

Celtic Sea

Isle of Wight

English Channel

Isles of Scilly

1 Which island lies off southern England?
2 Off which part of the British Isles can you see most islands?
3 Say where the Isle of Man is.
4 Which part of the British Isles has most large towns?

5 Is there more moorland in eastern or western Ireland?
6 Which part of Britain is nearest to southeast Ireland?
7 What can you find out from the map that the satellite photo does not show?

23

England and Wales

Town

Farmland

Forest and woodland

Moorland

These photos show the four main ways that land is used in the British Isles.
The moorland and forest and woodland areas are found in the hilly and mountainous parts of these islands.

Much of the British Isles is farmland, where cereal crops, fruit and vegetables are grown, and where cattle and sheep graze. The town environment includes not only places where people live but also where they work and shop.

Legend:
- Moorland
- Forest and woodland
- Farmland
- Town
- ⊕ Main airport
- Motorway
- Main road
- Railway
- National boundary
- River

1 centimetre on the map measures 25 kilometres on the ground.

Map labels:
Berwick-upon-Tweed, Newcastle, Sunderland, Middlesbrough, Yorkshire Moors, Scarborough, Hartlepool, Darlington, Harrogate, York, A1(M), Durham, Cheviot Hills, Hawick, Carlisle, Penrith, PENNINES, Lancaster, M6, SOUTHERN UPLANDS, Dumfries, LAKE DISTRICT, Scafell Pike, Morecambe Bay, Solway Firth, Workington, Barrow-in-Furness, Motherwell, Hamilton, Kilmarnock, M74, SCOTLAND, Ayr, Firth of Clyde, Arran, Douglas, Isle of Man, Islay, Stranraer, North Channel, Bangor, Belfast, NORTHERN IRELAND, M2, Mourne Mts., Slieve Donard, Coleraine, Ballymena, Portadown, Newry, M1, Dundalk Bay, REPUBLIC

24

25

Scotland

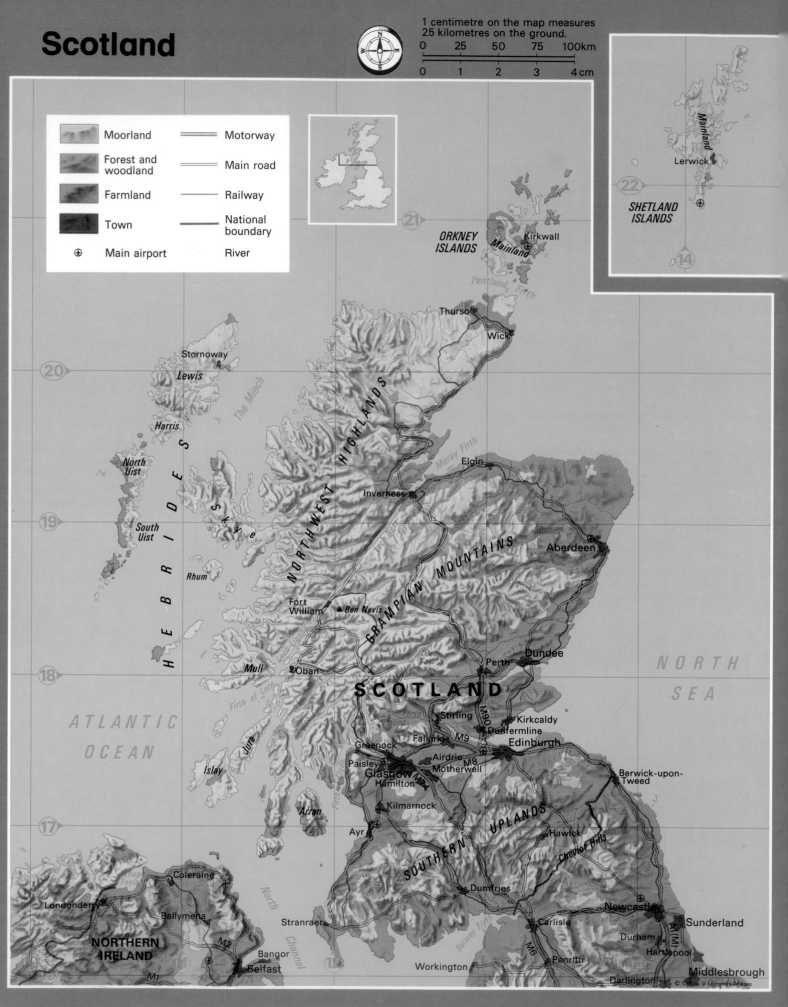

1 centimetre on the map measures
25 kilometres on the ground.

Moorland	Motorway
Forest and woodland	Main road
Farmland	Railway
Town	National boundary
⊕ Main airport	River

SHETLAND ISLANDS

Lerwick

ORKNEY ISLANDS

Mainland

Kirkwall

Pentland Firth

Thurso

Wick

Stornoway

Lewis

The Minch

NORTHWEST HIGHLANDS

Harris

North Uist

SKYE

South Uist

HEBRIDES

Rhum

Moray Firth

Elgin

Inverness

Loch Ness

GRAMPIAN MOUNTAINS

Aberdeen

Fort William

▲ Ben Nevis

Mull

Oban

Firth of Lorn

Jura

SCOTLAND

Perth

Dundee

Stirling

Kirkcaldy

Dunfermline

Falkirk

Edinburgh

M90

M9

ATLANTIC OCEAN

Islay

Greenock

Paisley

Airdrie

Motherwell

M8

Glasgow

Hamilton

Berwick-upon-Tweed

Arran

Kilmarnock

Ayr

SOUTHERN UPLANDS

Hawick

Cheviot Hills

NORTH SEA

Coleraine

Londonderry

Ballymena

Stranraer

Dumfries

Newcastle

Sunderland

NORTHERN IRELAND

Bangor

Belfast

M2

M1

Carlisle

Durham

Hartlepool

Penrith

M6

A(M)

Workington

Darlington

Middlesbrough

North Channel

Solway Firth

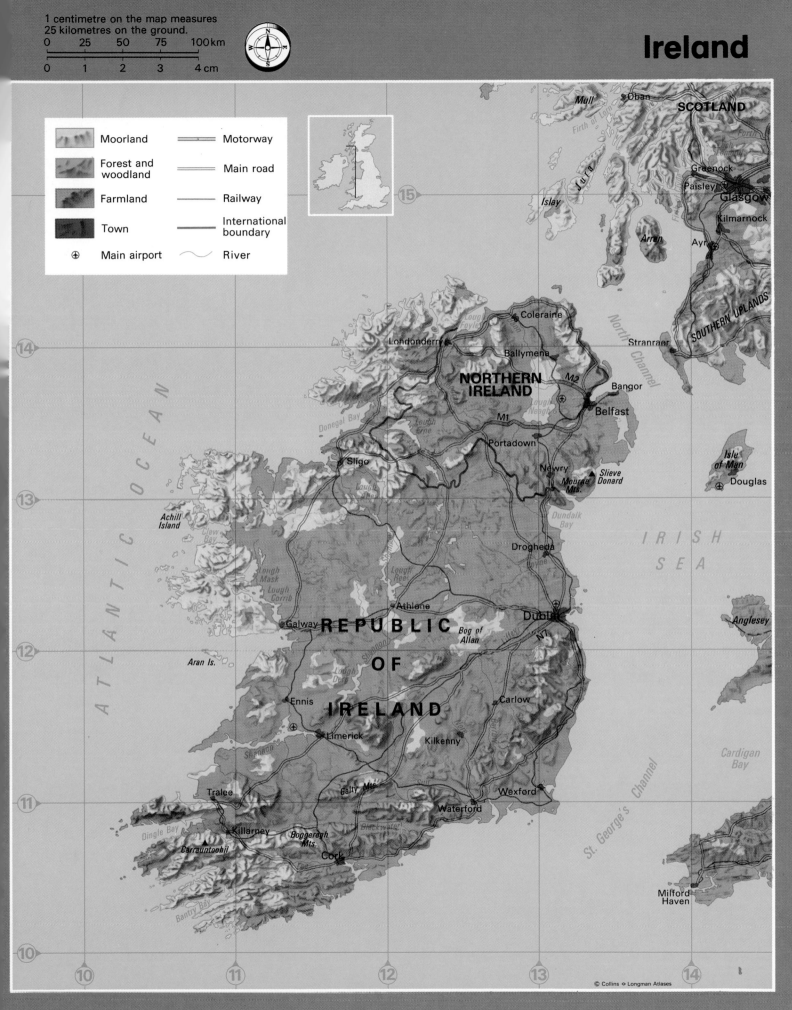

Ireland

1 centimetre on the map measures
25 kilometres on the ground.

0   25   50   75   100km

0   1   2   3   4 cm

Legend:
- Moorland
- Forest and woodland
- Farmland
- Town
- Main airport
- Motorway
- Main road
- Railway
- International boundary
- River

SCOTLAND
Mull
Oban
Firth of Lorne
Jura
Islay
Arran
Greenock
Paisley
Glasgow
Kilmarnock
Ayr
SOUTHERN UPLANDS

Coleraine
Londonderry
Lough Foyle
Ballymena
Stranraer
Northern Channel
NORTHERN IRELAND
M2
Bangor
Belfast
Lough Neagh
Portadown
M1
Newry
Lough Erne
Mourne Mts.
Slieve Donard
Isle of Man
Douglas

Donegal Bay
Sligo
Lough
Dundalk Bay

Achill Island
Clew Bay
Lough Mask
Lough Corrib
Lough Ree
Drogheda
Boyne

IRISH SEA

Athlone
Galway
REPUBLIC
Shannon
Bog of Allan
Dublin
Liffey
N7
Anglesey

Aran Is.
OF
Lough Derg

IRELAND
Ennis
Carlow
Barrow
Cardigan Bay

Limerick
Kilkenny
Shannon
Suir
St. George's Channel

Galty Mts.
Wexford
Tralee
Blackwater
Waterford

Dingle Bay
Killarney
Boggeragh Mts.
Carrauntoohil
Cork

Bantry Bay

Milford Haven

ATLANTIC OCEAN

© Collins ○ Longman Atlases

British Isles   Towns and Transport

Legend:
- Motorway
- Main road
- Railway
- Ferry route
- • Ferry port
- ■ Container port
- ⊕ Airport
- • Town

Shetland Islands

Lerwick

Orkney Islands

Kirkwall

Thurso

Wick

To Orkney and the Faroe Islands

Thurso
Wick
Stornoway
Ullapool
Elgin
Kyle of Lochalsh
Inverness
Aberdeen
Mallaig
Fort William
Tobermory
Perth
Dundee
Oban
Stirling
Glasgow
Edinburgh
Berwick-upon-Tweed
Campbeltown
Ayr
Hawick
Londonderry
Larne
Dumfries
Newcastle
Sunderland
Sligo
Belfast
Stranraer
Workington
Carlisle
Middlesbrough
Scarborough
Douglas
Barrow-in-Furness
Dundalk
Lancaster
York
Westport
Drogheda
Bradford
Leeds
Hull
Blackpool
Preston
Grimsby
Galway
Athlone
Liverpool
Manchester
Doncaster
Dublin
Birkenhead
Sheffield
Bangor
Crewe
Stoke
Nottingham
King's Lynn
Derby
Norwich
Limerick
Shrewsbury
Telford
Leicester
Great Yarmouth
Wolverhampton
Tralee
Birmingham
Rugby
Northampton
Ipswich
Killarney
Wexford
Aberystwyth
Coventry
Waterford
Worcester
Cambridge
Milton Keynes
Cork
Luton
Oxford
Merthyr Tydfil
Southend
Milford Haven
Swindon
London
Ramsgate
Swansea
Cardiff
Reading
Dover
Bristol
Folkestone
Taunton
Hastings
Southampton
Portsmouth
Exeter
Bournemouth
Weymouth
Plymouth
Torbay
Penzance

To Aberdeen
To Lerwick
To the Faroe Islands
To Iceland
To Scandinavia
To the Netherlands
To France
To the Channel Islands and France
To France and the Netherlands
To Spain

© Collins ○ Longman Atlases

British Isles   Counties and Regions

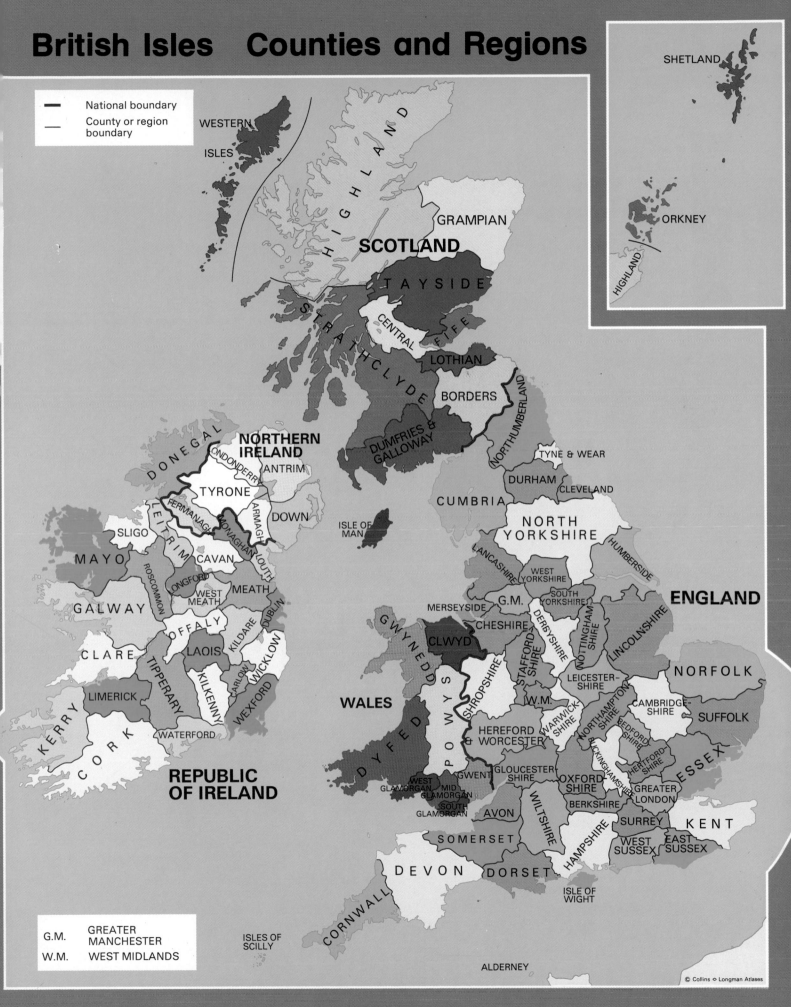

Legend:
- **National boundary**
- County or region boundary

SHETLAND

ORKNEY

HIGHLAND

WESTERN ISLES

HIGHLAND

GRAMPIAN

SCOTLAND

TAYSIDE

STRATHCLYDE

CENTRAL

FIFE

LOTHIAN

BORDERS

DUMFRIES & GALLOWAY

NORTHUMBERLAND

TYNE & WEAR

DURHAM

CLEVELAND

CUMBRIA

NORTH YORKSHIRE

HUMBERSIDE

LANCASHIRE

WEST YORKSHIRE

G.M.

SOUTH YORKSHIRE

ISLE OF MAN

DONEGAL

NORTHERN IRELAND

LONDONDERRY

ANTRIM

TYRONE

DOWN

FERMANAGH

ARMAGH

MONAGHAN

LOUTH

SLIGO

LEITRIM

CAVAN

MAYO

ROSCOMMON

LONGFORD

WEST MEATH

MEATH

GALWAY

OFFALY

KILDARE

DUBLIN

CLARE

LAOIS

WICKLOW

CARLOW

TIPPERARY

KILKENNY

WEXFORD

LIMERICK

KERRY

CORK

WATERFORD

REPUBLIC OF IRELAND

MERSEYSIDE

CHESHIRE

DERBYSHIRE

NOTTINGHAMSHIRE

LINCOLNSHIRE

STAFFORDSHIRE

LEICESTERSHIRE

W.M.

WARWICKSHIRE

NORTHAMPTONSHIRE

BEDFORDSHIRE

CAMBRIDGESHIRE

NORFOLK

SUFFOLK

ENGLAND

GWYNEDD

CLWYD

POWYS

SHROPSHIRE

WALES

DYFED

HEREFORD & WORCESTER

GWENT

GLOUCESTERSHIRE

OXFORDSHIRE

BUCKINGHAMSHIRE

HERTFORDSHIRE

GREATER LONDON

ESSEX

WEST GLAMORGAN

MID GLAMORGAN

SOUTH GLAMORGAN

AVON

WILTSHIRE

BERKSHIRE

SURREY

KENT

SOMERSET

HAMPSHIRE

WEST SUSSEX

EAST SUSSEX

DEVON

DORSET

ISLE OF WIGHT

CORNWALL

ISLES OF SCILLY

ALDERNEY

G.M.   GREATER MANCHESTER

W.M.   WEST MIDLANDS

© Collins ● Longman Atlases

29

British Isles Agriculture and Fishing

Hill farming

Mixed farming (mainly crops)

Mixed farming (mainly animals)

Mixed farming (mainly dairying)

Market gardening

Forest and woodland

Towns

Fishing ground

British Isles   Recreation

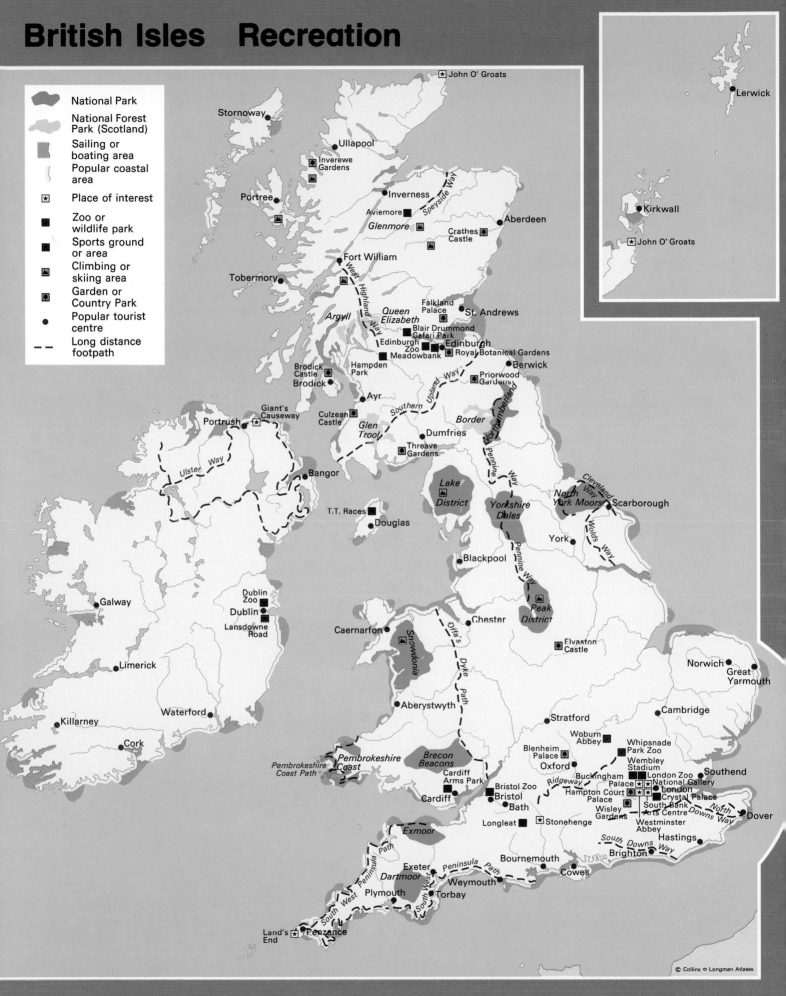

Legend

- National Park
- National Forest Park (Scotland)
- Sailing or boating area
- Popular coastal area
- ★ Place of interest
- ■ Zoo or wildlife park
- ■ Sports ground or area
- ▲ Climbing or skiing area
- ✦ Garden or Country Park
- ● Popular tourist centre
- - - Long distance footpath

Places and features labelled on the map:

Lerwick

Kirkwall
John O' Groats

★ John O' Groats
Stornoway
Ullapool
Inverewe Gardens
Portree
Inverness
Aviemore
Glenmore
Crathes Castle
Aberdeen
Speyside Way
Fort William
West Highland Way
Tobermory
Argyll
Queen Elizabeth
Falkland Palace
St. Andrews
Blair Drummond Safari Park
Edinburgh Zoo
Edinburgh
Meadowbank
Royal Botanical Gardens
Berwick
Brodick Castle
Brodick
Hampden Park
Priorwood Gardens
Ayr
Southern Upland Way
Border
Northumberland
Giant's Causeway
Portrush
Culzean Castle
Glen Trool
Dumfries
Threave Gardens
Pennine Way
Ulster Way
Bangor
Lake District
North York Moors
Cleveland Way
Scarborough
Yorkshire Dales
T.T. Races
Douglas
York
Wolds Way
Blackpool
Pennine Way
Peak District
Galway
Dublin Zoo
Dublin
Lansdowne Road
Chester
Caernarfon
Snowdonia
Offa's Dyke Path
Elvaston Castle
Limerick
Norwich
Great Yarmouth
Waterford
Aberystwyth
Stratford
Cambridge
Killarney
Cork
Pembrokeshire Coast Path
Pembrokeshire Coast
Brecon Beacons
Woburn Abbey
Blenheim Palace
Whipsnade Park Zoo
Wembley Stadium
Oxford
Cardiff Arms Park
Bristol Zoo
Ridgeway
Buckingham Palace
London Zoo
National Gallery
Southend
Cardiff
Bristol
Bath
Hampton Court Palace
London
Crystal Palace
Dover
Longleat
Stonehenge
Wisley Gardens
South Bank Arts Centre
Westminster Abbey
North Downs Way
Exmoor
Hastings
South Downs Way
Brighton
Bournemouth
Cowes
Exeter
Peninsula Path
Weymouth
Dartmoor
South West Peninsula Path
Torbay
Plymouth
Land's End
Penzance

© Collins ◇ Longman Atlases

British Isles Resources and Power

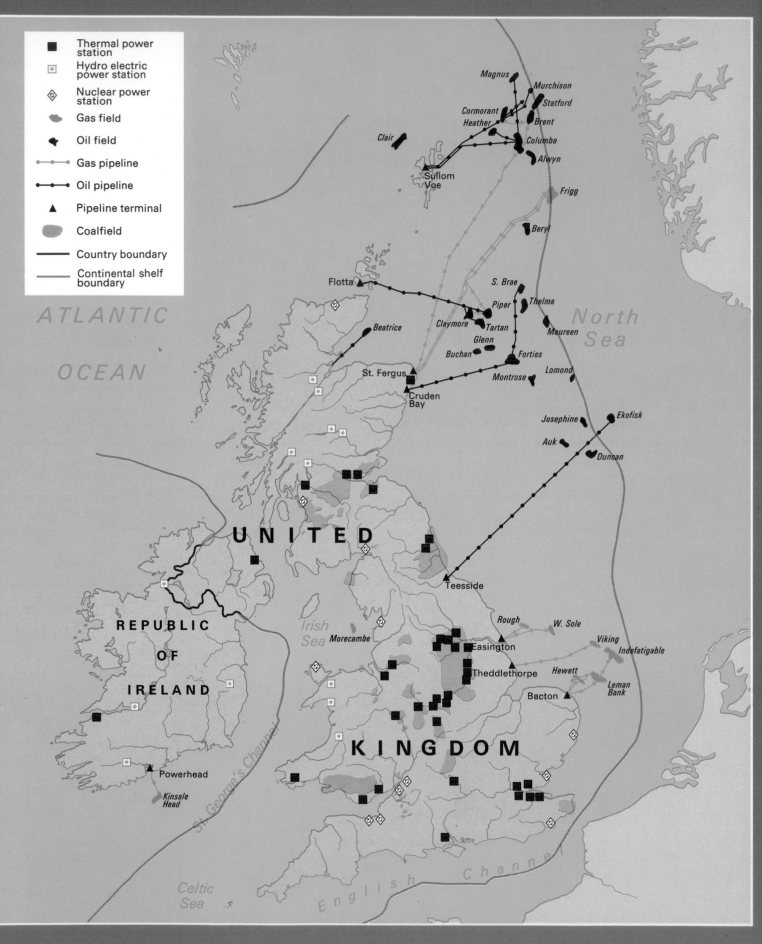

Legend:
- ■ Thermal power station
- ✳ Hydro electric power station
- ◇ Nuclear power station
- Gas field
- Oil field
- Gas pipeline
- Oil pipeline
- ▲ Pipeline terminal
- Coalfield
- Country boundary
- Continental shelf boundary

ATLANTIC OCEAN

North Sea

Magnus
Murchison
Statford
Cormorant
Heather
Brent
Clair
Columba
Alwyn
Sullom Voe
Frigg
Beryl

Flotta
S. Brae
Piper
Thelma
Claymore
Tartan
Maureen
Beatrice
Glenn
Buchan
Forties
St. Fergus
Montrose
Lomond
Cruden Bay
Josephine
Ekofisk
Auk
Duncan

UNITED

Teesside

Rough
W. Sole
Morecambe
Irish Sea
Viking
Indefatigable
Easington
Theddlethorpe
Hewett
Leman Bank
Bacton

REPUBLIC OF IRELAND

KINGDOM

Powerhead
Kinsale Head

St. George's Channel

Celtic Sea

English Channel

British Isles Industries and Services

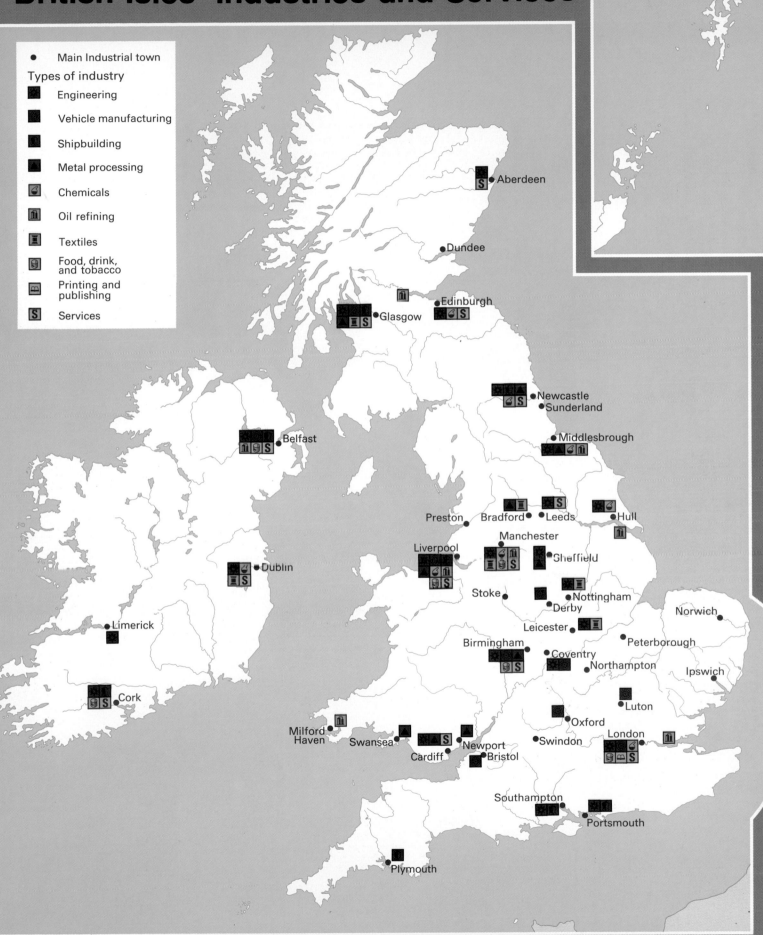

Main Industrial town •

Types of industry

- Engineering
- Vehicle manufacturing
- Shipbuilding
- Metal processing
- Chemicals
- Oil refining
- Textiles
- Food, drink, and tobacco
- Printing and publishing
- S Services

Aberdeen
Dundee
Edinburgh
Glasgow
Newcastle
Sunderland
Middlesbrough
Belfast
Preston
Bradford
Leeds
Hull
Liverpool
Manchester
Sheffield
Stoke
Nottingham
Derby
Dublin
Leicester
Norwich
Limerick
Birmingham
Coventry
Peterborough
Northampton
Ipswich
Cork
Luton
Milford Haven
Oxford
Swansea
Newport
London
Cardiff
Bristol
Swindon
Southampton
Portsmouth
Plymouth

Europe from Space

Below is a satellite photo of part of the continent of
Europe. This photo gives us a picture of what the
continent is like, but it does not show where the
countries are.

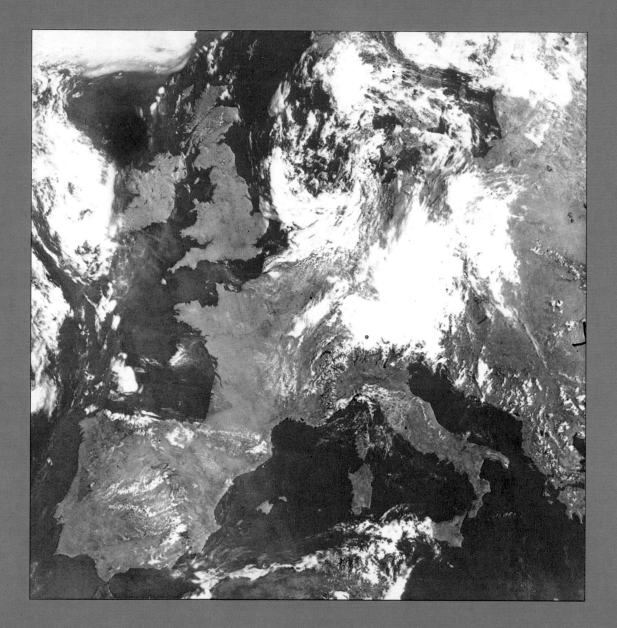

On a map, the boundaries can be drawn in. The map
opposite is a thematic map which shows each
country in Europe. It also shows the capital of each
country. The capital is the city where the government
of a country meets.

Europe   Countries and Capitals

1 centimetre on the map measures
200 kilometres on the ground.

| 0 | 200 | 400 | 600 | 800 | 1000 km |
| 0 | 1 | 2 | 3 | 4 | 5 cm |

ATLANTIC
OCEAN

ICELAND
Reykjavik

NORWAY
Oslo

SWEDEN
Stockholm

FINLAND
Helsinki

NORTH
SEA

Moscow

U.S.S.R.

REPUBLIC
OF
IRELAND
Dublin

UNITED
KINGDOM
London

DENMARK
Copenhagen

POLAND
Warsaw

Berlin
EAST
GERMANY

Amsterdam
NETHERLANDS
Brussels
BELGIUM
Bonn
LUXEMBOURG

Prague
CZECHOSLOVAKIA

Paris

WEST
GERMANY

Vienna
LIECHTENSTEIN
AUSTRIA

Budapest
HUNGARY

FRANCE

Berne
SWITZER-
LAND

Bay of
Biscay

PORTUGAL
Lisbon

SPAIN
Madrid

ANDORRA

MONACO

ITALY

SAN
MARINO

Corsica

Rome

YUGOSLAVIA

Belgrade

ROMANIA
Bucharest

Black Sea

Sofia
BULGARIA

ALBANIA
Tirane

TURKEY

Sardinia

GREECE

Mediterranean

Sicily

MALTA

Athens

Crete

Sea

Member of the E.E.C.
(European Economic Community)

Member of E.F.T.A.
(European Free Trade Association)

Member of COMECON
(Council for Mutual Economic Assistance)

Country which is not a member of
any of the above groups

■ Capital city

© Collins ○ Longman Atlases

Northern Europe

1 centimetre on the map measures
100 kilometres on the ground.

| 0 | 100 | 200 | 300 | 400 | 500 km |
| 0 | 1 | 2 | 3 | 4 | 5 cm |

Legend

- Ice and snow
- Tundra
- High mountains
- Desert
- Grassland
- Forest and woodland
- Farmland
- Industrial land with many people
- ■ Very large town (more than one million people)
- ● Large town (less than one million people)
- ⊕ Main airport
- Main road
- Railway
- River
- International boundary

ICELAND
Reykjavík
Mt. Hekla

Arctic Circle

ATLANTIC OCEAN

Faroe Is.

Shetland Is.

Orkney Is.

Hebrides

NORWAY
Bodø
Trondheim
Snøhetta
Glittertind
Bergen
Stavanger
Oslo

SWEDEN
Sund
Upp
Väste
Örebro
Norrk
Linkö
Göteborg
Borås
Jönköping
Vänern

NORTH SEA

Inverness
Aberdeen
Ben Nevis
Dundee
Glasgow
Edinburgh
Newcastle
Belfast
Middlesbrough
UNITED
REPUBLIC
OF
IRELAND
Dublin
Cork
KINGDOM
Liverpool
Leeds
Hull
Manchester
Sheffield
Birmingham
Coventry
Cardiff
Bristol
London
Southampton
Plymouth

English Channel

Älborg
Århus
Esbjerg
DENMARK
Hälsingborg
Copenhagen
Odense
Malmö
Kiel
Rostock
Hamburg
Schwerin
Bremen
Szczecin
NETHERLANDS
Amsterdam
Enschede
Rotterdam
Hannover
EAST
Berlin
Utrecht
Magdeburg
WEST
Calais
Antwerp
Dortmund
GERMANY
Gent
Düsseldorf
Halle
Poz
Lille
Brussels
Cologne
GERMANY
Leipzig
Dresden
Lens
Liège
Bonn
Wrocław
BELGIUM
Le Havre
Karl Marx Stadt
Oder

© Collins ⊙ Longman Atlases

Hammerfest

Kiruna

Murmansk

Kirovsk

Mezen

Naryan Mar

Ust'Tsilma

Troitsko Pechorsk

F I N L A N D

White Sea

Luleå
Kemi
Oulu

Arkhangel'sk

Severodvinsk

Syktyvkar

Vaasa

Kuopio

Petrozavodsk

Kotlas

Kirov

Tampere

Lappeenranta

Lahti

L. Ladoga

ckholm

Turku

Helsinki

Gulf of Finland

Leningrad

Cherepovets
Vologda

Kostroma

Kineshma

Yoshkar Ola

Tallinn

Novgorod

Andropov

Ivanovo

Gorki

Cheboksary

Kazan

Yaroslavl

Dzherzhinsk

Pskov

Kalinin

Vladimir

Murom

Ul'yanovsk

Riga

Velikiye-Luki

Khimki

Moscow

Orekhovo-Zuyevo

Saransk

Tol'yatti

Daugavpils

Dvina

Kolomna

Syzran

Klaipeda

Vitebsk

Kaluga

Ryazan

Penza

Balakovo

Kaunas

Vilnius

Orsha

Tula

Michurinsk

Tambov

Saratov

Engels

ynia
Kaliningrad

Mogilev

Minsk

Bryansk

Orel

Lipetsk

nsk

Grodno

U.

U.

S.

S.

R.

oszoz

Baranovichi

Gomel

Voronezh

Kamyshin

Toruń

Bialystok

Kursk

LAND

Warsaw

Brest

Pripet Marshes

Chernigov

Sumy

Belgorod

ź

Radom

Lublin

Rovno

Zhitomir

Kiev

Kharkov

Poltava

Volzhskiy

Volgograd

Southern Europe

POLAND
Warsaw
Brest
Łódź
Radom
Lublin
Zabrze
Katowice
Ostrava
Cracow
SLOVAKIA
Košice
Bratislava
Miskolc
Budapest
HUNGARY
Szeged
Pécs
Debrecen
Novi Sad
Timişoara
Belgrade
YUGOSLAVIA
Sarajevo
Split
Niš
Sofia
Bari
ALBANIA
Tiranë
Thessaloniki
Mt. Olympus ▲
GREECE
Vólos
Pátras
Athens

Carpathians

Chernovtsy
ROMANIA
Sibiu
Braşov
Craiova
Bucharest
Ploieşti
Ruse
BULGARIA
Skopje
Plovdiv
Burgas
Varna
Constanţa

Rovno
Lvov
Khmelnitskiy
Vinnitsa
Kishinev
Iaşi
Tiraspol
Galaţi
Odessa

Zhitomir
Kiev
Cherkassy
Kirovograd
Dneprodzerzhinsk
Krivoy Rog
Nikopol
Nikolayev
Kherson

Chernigov
Sumy
U.S.S.R.
Poltava
Dnepropetrovsk
Donetsk

Belgorod
Kharkov
Lisichansk
Voroshilovgrad
Gorlovka
Shakhty
Makéyevka
Rostov
Taganrog
Zhdanov

Volgograd

Sea of Azov
Kerch
Simferopol'
Sevastopol'
Novorossiysk
Krasnodar
Armavir
Maykop
Sochi
Sukhumi

Black Sea

Danube

Istanbul
TURKEY
ASIA

Aegean

Ionian Sea

Rhodes

Crete
Iráklion

SEA

© Collins ◇ Longman Atlases

Weather maps

(A) BRITISH ISLES

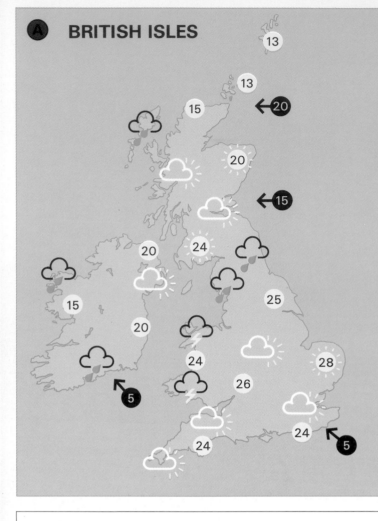

We all like to know what the weather will be like tomorrow. Every day the weather forecast is given on television on a map like map **A** of the British Isles. On map **A**, symbols are used to explain what the weather may be like in each part of the country. The key shows what the symbols mean. The satellite photo **B**, shows how cloudy it was on the day for which the forecast was made.

☀ 24	Sunshine, highest temperature in degrees centigrade
☁☀	Cloudy with sunny spells
☁☂	Rain
☁⚡	Thunderstorms
20	Highest temperature in degrees centigrade
↖ 8	Wind direction and speed

WEATHER

London, SE, central S, E, NW, central N, NE England, East Anglia, E, W Midlands, N Wales, Lake District: A few sunny intervals but thundery showers at times; wind SE light; max temp 25°C (77°F).

Channel Islands, SW England, S Wales: Sunny intervals, scattered showers developing, perhaps thundery; wind mainly SE light; max temp 22°C (72°F).

Isle of Man, SW Scotland, Glasgow, central Highlands, Moray Firth, Argyll, Northern Ireland: Some sunny intervals, isolated thundery showers; wind mainly E light; max temp 24°C (75°F).

Borders, Edinburgh, Dundee, Aberdeen: Mainly cloudy but a few sunny intervals developing away from coasts; wind E moderate; max temp 19°C (66°F).

NE, NW Scotland, Orkney, Shetland: Rather cloudy with outbreaks of rain and drizzle in places; wind E moderate; max temp 18°C (64°F).

Outlook for tomorrow and Saturday: Unsettled, with thundery showers in most areas, but also some sunny intervals; remaining very warm in sunnier areas.

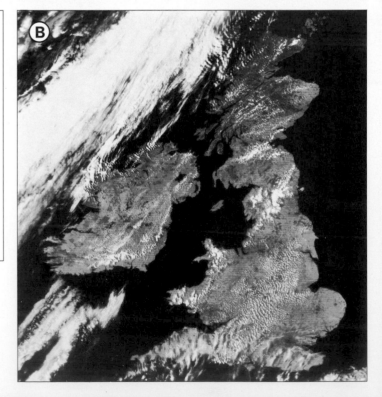

? 1 What was the weather like in Scotland?
2 Which part of England does the satellite photo **B** show had no cloud?
3 Is the newspaper forecast for Wales the same as the weather map forecast?

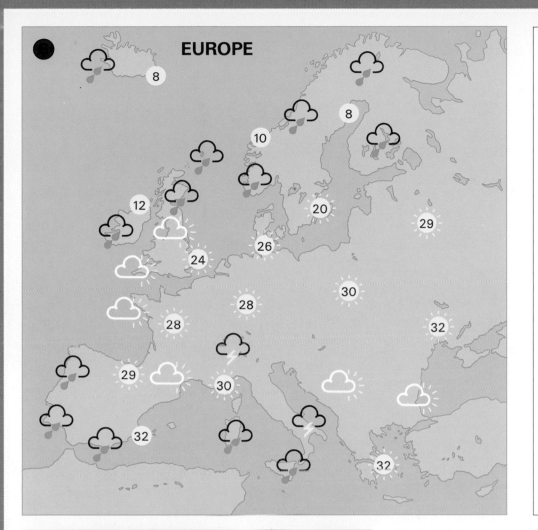

EUROPE

EUROPE

		C	F
Amsterdam	s	27	81
Athens	s	31	88
Barcelona	f	28	82
Belgrade	f	29	84
Berlin	s	28	82
Biarritz	c	29	84
Boulogne	c	24	75
Bordeaux	s	27	81
Brussels	s	25	77
Budapest	f	30	86
Cologne	s	27	81
Copenhagen	s	23	73
Dublin	c	18	64
Dubrovnik	s	25	77
Florence	c	29	84
Frankfurt	s	28	82
Geneva	f	26	79
Helsinki	f	18	64
Innsbruck	c	25	77
Lisbon	c	28	82
Locarno	c	26	79
Luxemburg	s	28	82
Madrid	c	30	86
Majorca	f	28	82
Malaga	s	30	86
Milan	s	29	84
Moscow	s	30	86
Munich	f	26	79
Naples	c	27	81
Nice	s	30	86
Oslo	c	18	64
Paris	s	24	75
Prague	s	28	82
Reykjavik	c	11	52
Rome	c	27	81
Salzburg	s	28	82
Stockholm	s	21	70
Strasbourg	s	28	82
Venice	s	30	86
Vienna	s	28	82
Warsaw	s	29	84

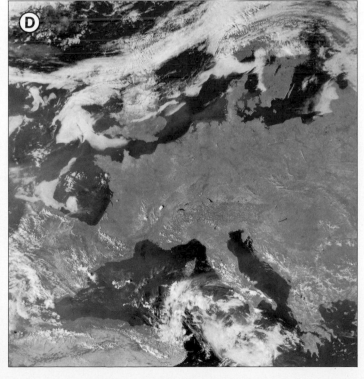

During the summer many people go to Europe for their holidays, so the weather forecaster uses a map of Europe like map **C** to show what the weather may be like over the whole of the continent. The chart shows how hot some of the main resorts were.

? Use the map on page 35 to help you with these questions.
1 Which parts of Europe does the satellite photo **D** show were cloudy?
2 Name three countries which would have had a clear sunny day.
3 Where in Europe were the hottest resorts?

The Earth from Space

B

C

NORTH AMERICA

+North Pole

ATLANTIC OCEAN

EUROPE

ASIA

AFRICA

INDIAN OCEAN

+ North Pole

EUROPE

ASIA

AFRICA

PACIFIC OCEAN

INDIAN OCEAN

AUSTRALASIA

One of the best known photos of Earth was taken from the spacecraft Apollo 11 on its way to the Moon in July 1969. It shows the Earth as a ball in space. The astronauts on Apollo 8 were the first people who actually saw this view of Earth. They had orbited the Moon over Christmas, 1968. But for over two thousand years it has been known that the Earth is round. In about 150 AD the Greek geographer Ptolemy described how to model the Earth as a sphere. Yet it is only in the last few hundred years that accurate models, called globes, have been made.

F

D

NORTH AMERICA

ATLANTIC OCEAN

PACIFIC OCEAN

SOUTH AMERICA

E

AUSTRALASIA

PACIFIC OCEAN

ANTARCTICA
South Pole

A globe is the only way to show the shape of all the features on the Earth accurately. These four pictures show how the continents look on a globe. The globe has been turned round in each picture so you can see the whole of each continent.

?

1 Which continent can you see all of in photo **A**?
2 Which continents are shown in picture **C**?
3 In which continent is the south pole?
4 How many continents are there?
5 Which continents surround the Pacific Ocean?

Countries of the World

1 centimetre on the map measures
850 kilometres on the ground.

0	850	1700	2550	3400	4250 km
0	1	2	3	4	5 cm

A map of the Earth has to show the whole of a sphere on flat paper. This cannot be done without changing the exact shape or size of the continents and oceans either slightly or quite a lot.

DOM. REP. : DOMINICAN REPUBLIC
E.S. : EL SALVADOR
JAM. : JAMAICA
P.R. : PUERTO RICO

D. : DJIBOUTI
EQ. G. : EQUATORIAL GUINEA
GAM. : GAMBIA
G. B. : GUINEA BISSAU
MAL. : MALAWI
ZIM. : ZIMBABWE

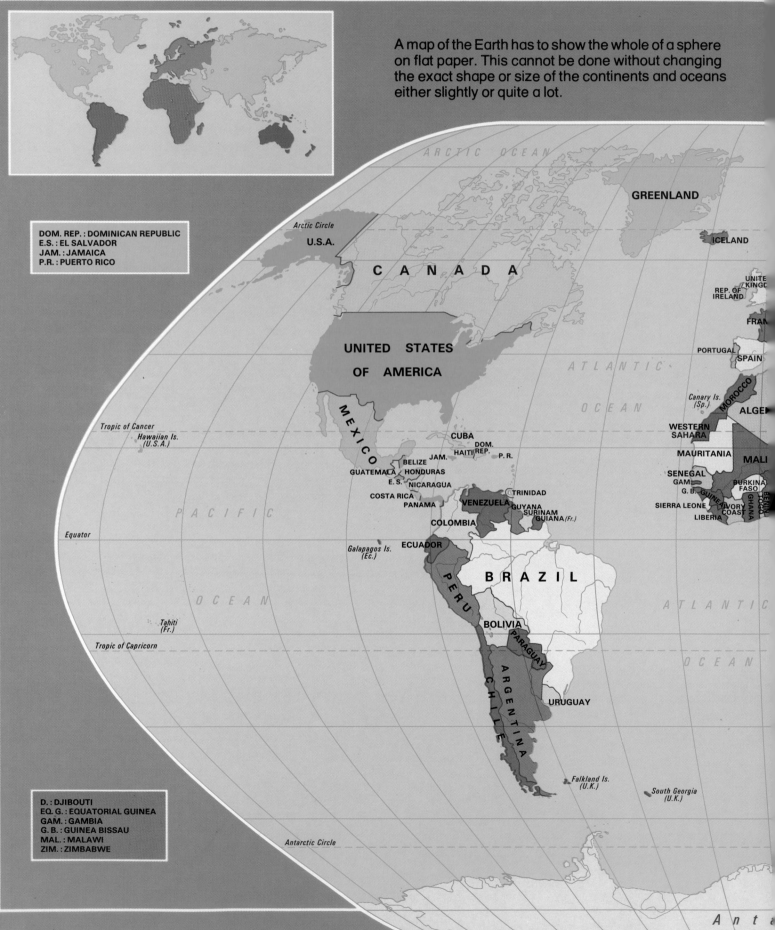

ARCTIC OCEAN

GREENLAND

ICELAND

Arctic Circle

U.S.A.

C A N A D A

REP. OF
IRELAND

UNITE
KINGD

FRAN

PORTUGAL

SPAIN

ATLANTIC

OCEAN

UNITED STATES
OF AMERICA

Canary Is.
(Sp.)

MOROCCO

ALGE

M E X I C O

Tropic of Cancer

Hawaiian Is.
(U.S.A.)

WESTERN
SAHARA

CUBA

DOM.
REP.

HAITI

P. R.

MAURITANIA

MALI

BELIZE

JAM.

SENEGAL

GUATEMALA

HONDURAS

GAM.

BURKINA
FASO

E.S.

NICARAGUA

G. B.

GUINE

IVORY
COAST

GHANA

BENIN
TOGO

COSTA RICA

SIERRA LEONE

PANAMA

TRINIDAD

LIBERIA

VENEZUELA

GUYANA

SURINAM

COLOMBIA

GUIANA (Fr.)

Galapagos Is.
(Ec.)

ECUADOR

Equator

P A C I F I C

B R A Z I L

ATLANTIC

P E R U

BOLIVIA

OCEAN

Tahiti
(Fr.)

PARAGUAY

Tropic of Capricorn

A R G E N T I N A

C H I L E

URUGUAY

OCEAN

OCEAN

Falkland Is.
(U.K.)

South Georgia
(U.K.)

Antarctic Circle

Ant

44

This map shows one way to draw the continents and oceans. The two small inset World maps show other ways this can be done. Can you spot the differences?

ARCTIC OCEAN

Arctic Circle

UNION OF SOVIET SOCIALIST REPUBLICS

Aleutian Is. (U.S.A.)

FINLAND

sbergen (Nor.)

ROMANIA
BULG.
GREECE
TURKEY
Black Sea
Caspian Sea
MONGOLIA
C H I N A
N. KOREA
S. KOREA
JAPAN

C.
LEB.
IS.
SYRIA
IRAQ
IRAN
AFGHAN-ISTAN
JAMMU & KASHMIR
JORDAN
KU.

ean Sea
EGYPT
SAUDI
ARABIA
U.A.E.
Q.
OMAN
PAKISTAN
NEPAL
BHUTAN
BANGL.
Tropic of Cancer
TAIWAN

HAD
SUDAN
YEMEN
SOUTHERN YEMEN
INDIA
BURMA
PACIFIC

ENTRAL RICAN
ETHIOPIA
SOMALI REP.
SRI LANKA
VIETNAM
THAI-LAND
KAM.
PHILIPPINES

UGANDA
KENYA
MALDIVES
MALAYSIA
BR.
SING.
OCEAN
Equator

ZAÏRE
RWANDA
BURUNDI
TANZANIA
SEYCHELLES
INDONESIA
PAPUA NEW GUINEA
KIRIBATI

GOLA
ZAMBIA
MAL.
MOZAMBIQUE
COMOROS
I N D I A N
SOLOMON IS.
VANUATU
FIJI

BIA
ZIM.
BOTSWANA
SWAZILAND
MADAGASCAR
OCEAN
AUSTRALIA
New Caledonia (Fr.)
TONGA
Tropic of Capricorn

REP. OF
LESOTHO
UTH AFRICA
NEW ZEALAND

Prince Edward Is. (R.S.A.)
Kerguelen (Fr.)

Antarctic Circle

tica

© Collins ◊ Longman Atlases

AL. : ALBANIA
AU. : AUSTRIA
B. : BELGIUM
BULG. : BULGARIA
CZ. : CZECHOSLOVAKIA
DEN. : DENMARK
E. GER. : EAST GERMANY
HUNG. : HUNGARY
L. : LUXEMBOURG
N. : NETHERLANDS
SW. : SWITZERLAND
W. GER. : WEST GERMANY
YUGO. : YUGOSLAVIA

BANGL. : BANGLADESH
BR. : BRUNEI
C. : CYPRUS
IS. : ISRAEL
KAM. : KAMPUCHEA
KU. : KUWAIT
LEB. : LEBANON
Q. : QATAR
SING. : SINGAPORE
U. A. E. : UNITED ARAB EMIRATES

Africa from space

This is a satellite photo of the continent of Africa. The map opposite shows both the environments of Africa and where the countries are in the continent. Some of the largest towns and cities have been named.

Africa

1 centimetre on the map measures 400 kilometres on the ground.

0	400	800	1200	1600	2000 km
0	1	2	3	4	5 cm

At the same scale

Legend

- High mountains
- Desert
- Grassland
- Forest and woodland
- Farmland
- Industrial land with many people
- ■ Very large town (more than one million people)
- ● Large town (less than one million people)
- —— International boundary

Labels on map:

EUROPE

ASIA

Mediterranean Sea

Canary Is.

WESTERN SAHARA

MOROCCO
Tetuan Oran Algiers Annaba Tunis
Rabat Fez Constantine
Casablanca
Marrakesh
TUNISIA Tripoli Sfax
Benghazi
Alexandria Port Said
El Giza Cairo

ALGERIA
LIBYA
EGYPT
Aswan

SAHARA DESERT

MAURITANIA
Nouakchott
MALI
NIGER
CHAD
SUDAN
Port Sudan
Omdurman
Khartoum Asmara
N'Djamena
Lake Chad
DJIBOUTI
Addis Ababa
ETHIOPIA
SOMALI REPUBLIC

Dakar SENEGAL
GAMBIA
GUINEA BISSAU
GUINEA
Conakry
SIERRA LEONE
LIBERIA
IVORY COAST
Bouaké
GHANA
Kumasi
Abidjan Accra
Bamako
Niamey
BURKINA FASO
Kano
NIGERIA
Ibadan Ogbomosho
Lagos
TOGO BENIN
CAMEROON
Douala
Yaoundé
EQUATORIAL GUINEA
GABON
CONGO
Brazzaville
Kinshasa
CENTRAL AFRICAN REPUBLIC
Bangui
Kisangani
ZAÏRE
Kananga
Mbuji Mayi
UGANDA
Kampala
KENYA
Nairobi
Mogadishu
Equator
RWANDA
BURUNDI
Mombasa
Kilimanjaro
TANZANIA
Dar es Salaam

Red Sea

White Nile
Blue Nile
Niger

ATLANTIC OCEAN

INDIAN OCEAN

Tropic of Cancer

Luanda
ANGOLA
Lubumbashi
Kitwe
Ndola
ZAMBIA
Lusaka
MALAWI
Blantyre
MOZAMBIQUE
Harare
ZIMBABWE
Bulawayo
NAMIBIA
Namib Desert
BOTSWANA
Kalahari Desert
Pretoria
Johannesburg
Maputo
SWAZILAND
LESOTHO
Durban
REPUBLIC OF SOUTH AFRICA
Cape Town
Port Elizabeth

MADAGASCAR
Antananarivo

Tropic of Capricorn

Mozambique Channel

Orange
Limpopo
Zambezi
Cubango
Kwango

© Collins ○ Longman Atlases

47

Grid references: A B C D E F G H (columns), 1–8 (rows)

Asia

1 centimetre on the map measures
400 kilometres on the ground

0	400	800	1200	1600	2000 km
0	1	2	3	4	5 cm

At the same scale

Legend

Ice and snow	
Tundra	
High mountains	
Desert	
Grassland	
Forest and woodland	
Farmland	
Industrial land with many people	
International boundary	
■	Very large town (more than one million people)
●	Large town (less than one million people)

Map labels

EUROPE

Minsk
Leningrad
Moscow
Gorki
Kiev Kharkov
Kazan
Perm
Donetsk
Odessa
Kuybyshev
Sverdlovsk
Volgograd
Chelyabinsk
Omsk
Novosibirsk
Irkutsk

UNION OF SOVIET SOCIALIST REPUBLICS

SIBERIA

Novaya Zemlya
Ural Mountains
Yenisey
Arctic Circle
Yakutsk
Harb...
Changchun
Ulan Bator

MONGOLIA

Gobi Desert
Shenyang
Karaganda
L. Balkash
Beijing
Lüda
Taiyuan Tianjin
Jinan
Qingdao
Zhengzhou

Istanbul
Ankara
TURKEY
CYPRUS
Tbilisi
Yerevan
Baku
Caucasus
Black Sea
Caspian Sea
Aral Sea
Tashkent
Alma-Ata
Ürümqi
Lanzhou
Xi'an
Nanjing
Wuhan

LEBANON
Tel Aviv-Yafo
ISRAEL
Damascus
SYRIA
IRAQ
JORDAN
Baghdad
KUWAIT
Kuwait
Tehran
Isfahan
IRAN
AFGHANISTAN
Kabul
JAMMU AND KASHMIR
Tibetan Plateau
CHINA
Chengdu
Chongqing
Changsha

SAUDI
ARABIA
BAHRAIN
QATAR
Riyadh
UNITED ARAB EMIRATES
Dubai
Muscat
OMAN
PAKISTAN
Lahore
Karachi
Indus
Delhi
Agra
Kanpur
NEPAL
BHUTAN
HIMALAYA
Mt. Everest
Kunming
Guangzhou
Kowloon
HONG KONG

YEMEN
San'a
SOUTHERN YEMEN
Aden
Ahmadabad
Varanasi
Ganges
Calcutta
Dhaka
BANGLADESH
BURMA
Hanoi
Haiphong
Hainan

Bombay
Pune
INDIA
Godavari
Hyderabad
Arabian Sea
Bay of Bengal
Rangoon
THAILAND
Bangkok
LAOS
VIETNAM
KAMPUCHEA
Phnom Penh
Ho Chi Minh City

Bangalore
Madras
Colombo
SRI LANKA
South China...

INDIAN OCEAN
Equator
MALAYSIA
Kuala Lumpur
SINGAPORE
Singapore
BRUNEI
Borneo
INDON...
Jakarta
Surabaya
Java
Bandung
Sumatra

48

These photos show the different environments on the maps on pages 47 to 57.

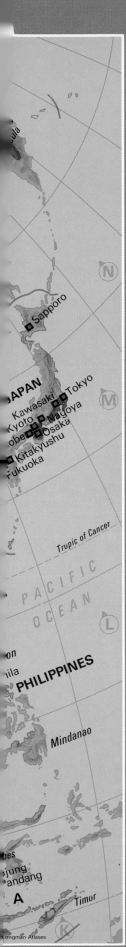

Ice and snow

Tundra

High mountains

Desert

Grassland

Forest and woodland

Farmland

Industrial land with many people

North America

1 centimetre on the map measures
400 kilometres on the ground.

| 0 | 400 | 800 | 1200 | 1600 | 2000 km |
| 0 | 1 | 2 | 3 | 4 | 5 cm |

At the same scale

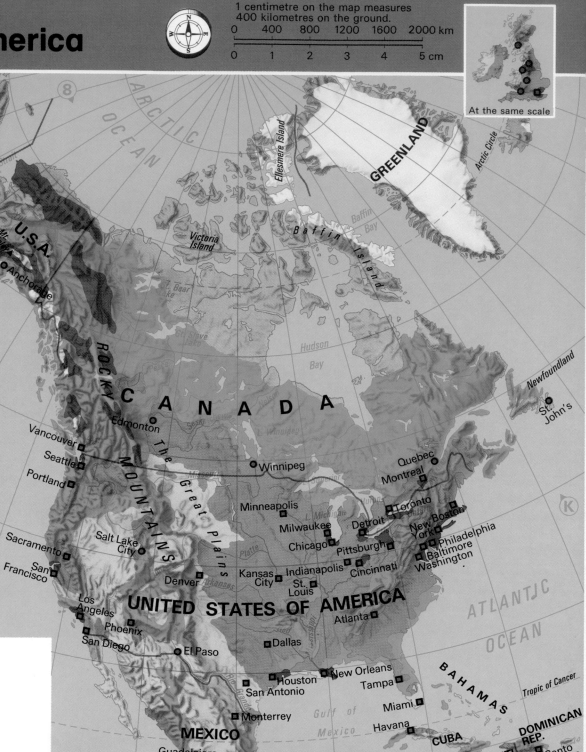

Legend

- Ice and snow
- Tundra
- High mountains
- Desert
- Grassland
- Forest and woodland
- Farmland
- Industrial land with many people
- ■ Very large town (more than one million people)
- ● Large town (less than one million people)
- — International boundary

ASIA

ARCTIC OCEAN

GREENLAND

Arctic Circle

U.S.A.

Mt. McKinley

Anchorage

Ellesmere Island

Baffin Bay

Baffin Island

Victoria Island

Bear Lake

Great Slave Lake

Hudson Bay

C A N A D A

Newfoundland

St. John's

Vancouver

Edmonton

Seattle

Portland

Winnipeg

Quebec

Montreal

ROCKY MOUNTAINS

The Great Plains

Minneapolis

Milwaukee

Detroit

Toronto

New York

Boston

Sacramento

Salt Lake City

Chicago

Pittsburgh

Philadelphia

Baltimore

Washington

San Francisco

Denver

Kansas City

Indianapolis

Cincinnati

St. Louis

Los Angeles

UNITED STATES OF AMERICA

Atlanta

ATLANTIC OCEAN

Phoenix

San Diego

El Paso

Dallas

New Orleans

BAHAMAS

Tropic of Cancer

Houston

San Antonio

Tampa

Miami

Monterrey

Gulf of Mexico

Havana

CUBA

DOMINICAN REP.

MEXICO

WEST INDIES

HAITI

Santo Domingo

Guadalajara

Kingston

JAMAICA

CARIBBEAN SEA

Mexico City

BELIZE

HONDURAS

Guatemala City

San Salvador

NICARAGUA

GUATEMALA

Managua

EL SALVADOR

Panama City

COSTA RICA

PANAMA

SOUTH AMERICA

Equator

PACIFIC OCEAN

© Collins · Longman Atlases

50

South America

1 centimetre on the map measures
400 kilometres on the ground.

0   400   800   1200   1600   2000 km
0   1   2   3   4   5 cm

At the same scale

Ice and snow

Tundra

High mountains

Desert

Grassland

Forest and woodland

Farmland

Industrial land with many people

■ Very large town (more than one million people)

● Large town (less than one million people)

— International boundary

Tropic of Cancer

ATLANTIC OCEAN

WEST INDIES

Caribbean Sea

CENTRAL AMERICA

Barranquilla   Maracaibo   Valencia
Cartagena   Caracas   **TRINIDAD**
Bucaramanga   **VENEZUELA**   Georgetown
Medellin   **GUYANA**   Paramaribo
Cali   **COLOMBIA**   **SURINAM**
                                     FRENCH GUIANA
Quito
ECUADOR
Guayaquil   Belém
                          Manaus   São Luís
Iquitos   Fortaleza
                                    Teresina   Natal
Trujillo   **P E R U**   **B R A Z I L**   Recife
                                              Maceió
Callao   Aracaju
Lima   Salvador
Arequipa   Brasília
                            Goiânia
La Paz
BOLIVIA
Sucre   Belo Horizonte
                                        Campinas   Campos
PARAGUAY   Londrina   São Paulo   Niterói
Antofagasta   Santos   Rio de Janeiro
                          Asunción   Curitiba
                                      Pôrto Alegre
Córdoba
Mendoza   Rosario   **URUGUAY**
Valparaíso   Buenos   Montevideo
Santiago   Aires
Mt. Aconcagua
Concepción   Mar del Plata

C H I L E   **A R G E N T I N A**   **A N D E S**

PACIFIC OCEAN

Equator

Tropic of Capricorn

SOUTH ATLANTIC OCEAN

Falkland Is.

Punta Arenas
Tierra del Fuego

© Collins ◇ Longman Atlases

51

Australasia

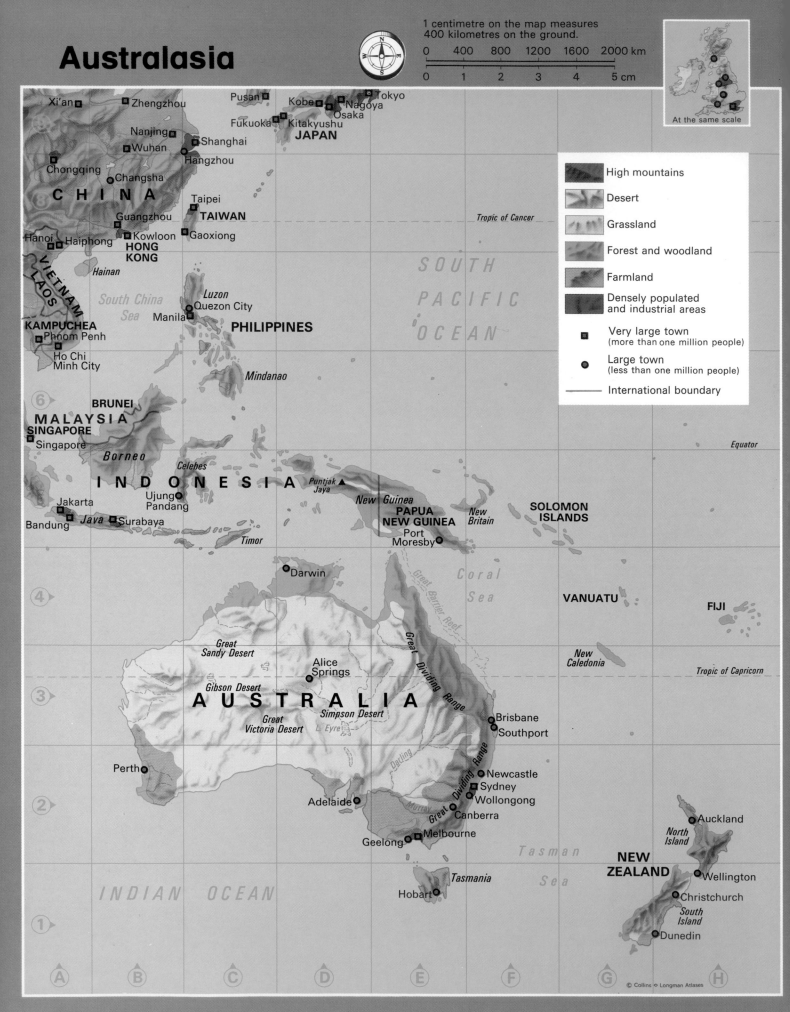

1 centimetre on the map measures
400 kilometres on the ground.

| 0 | 400 | 800 | 1200 | 1600 | 2000 km |

| 0 | 1 | 2 | 3 | 4 | 5 cm |

At the same scale

Legend:
- High mountains
- Desert
- Grassland
- Forest and woodland
- Farmland
- Densely populated and industrial areas
- ■ Very large town (more than one million people)
- ● Large town (less than one million people)
- International boundary

Tropic of Cancer

SOUTH PACIFIC OCEAN

CHINA
Xi'an
Zhengzhou
Nanjing
Wuhan
Shanghai
Chongqing
Changsha
Hangzhou
Guangzhou
Taipei
TAIWAN
Gaoxiong
Hanoi
Haiphong
Kowloon
HONG KONG
Hainan
VIETNAM
LAOS
KAMPUCHEA
Phnom Penh
Ho Chi Minh City
South China Sea

Pusan
Kobe
Nagoya
Tokyo
Fukuoka
Kitakyushu
Osaka
JAPAN

BRUNEI
MALAYSIA
SINGAPORE
Singapore
Borneo

Luzon
Quezon City
Manila
PHILIPPINES
Mindanao

Celebes
INDONESIA
Ujung Pandang
Jakarta
Java
Surabaya
Bandung
Timor

Puntjak Jaya ▲
New Guinea
PAPUA NEW GUINEA
Port Moresby
New Britain

SOLOMON ISLANDS

Equator

VANUATU

FIJI

New Caledonia

Tropic of Capricorn

Coral Sea

Darwin

Great Sandy Desert
Gibson Desert
Great Victoria Desert
Great Dividing Range
Alice Springs
Simpson Desert
L. Eyre
AUSTRALIA
Darling
Perth
Adelaide
Murray
Brisbane
Southport
Newcastle
Sydney
Wollongong
Canberra
Melbourne
Geelong
Tasmania
Hobart

Tasman Sea

NEW ZEALAND
North Island
Auckland
Wellington
Christchurch
South Island
Dunedin

INDIAN OCEAN

Ⓐ Ⓑ Ⓒ Ⓓ Ⓔ Ⓕ Ⓖ Ⓗ

© Collins ◆ Longman Atlases

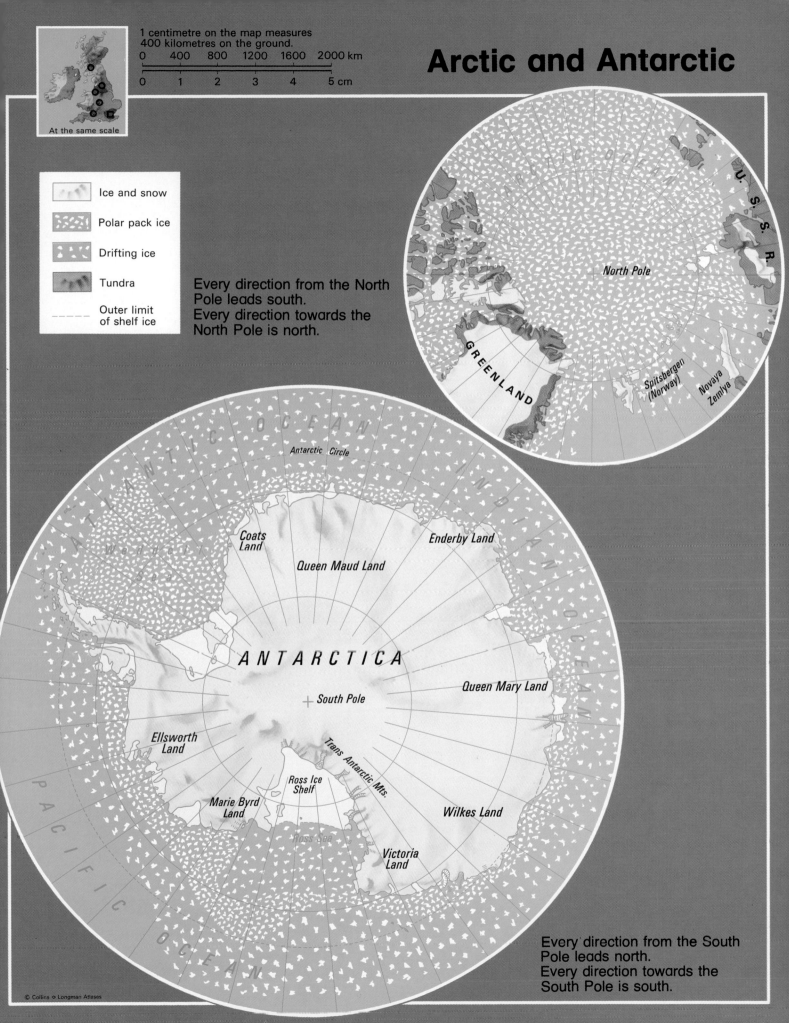

1 centimetre on the map measures
400 kilometres on the ground.

0	400	800	1200	1600	2000 km

0	1	2	3	4	5 cm

At the same scale

Ice and snow

Polar pack ice

Drifting ice

Tundra

Outer limit
of shelf ice

Every direction from the North
Pole leads south.
Every direction towards the
North Pole is north.

North Pole

U. S. S. R.

GREENLAND

Spitsbergen
(Norway)

Novaya
Zemlya

ARCTIC OCEAN

Antarctic Circle

Coats
Land

Queen Maud Land

Enderby Land

ATLANTIC OCEAN

INDIAN OCEAN

A N T A R C T I C A

+ South Pole

Queen Mary Land

Ellsworth
Land

Trans Antarctic Mts.

Ross Ice
Shelf

Marie Byrd
Land

Wilkes Land

Ross Sea

Victoria
Land

PACIFIC OCEAN

Every direction from the South
Pole leads north.
Every direction towards the
South Pole is south.

© Collins ◦ Longman Atlases

53

The Caribbean

The Caribbean is the name given to the area of sea and islands between the continents of North and South America. On these pages you can see a map showing the sea and many of the islands. Compare the sizes of the islands with the inset map of England and Wales. You will see that some of the islands are smaller than the Isle of Wight off England's south coast, and that two islands are larger than Wales. In fact, Cuba is almost as large in area as England. This map of the Caribbean is drawn at the same scale as the maps of Europe on pages 36 to 39. You can see how great the distances are between the islands. The plan of central Kingston, Jamaica's capital, is drawn at the same scale as map **C** on page 5.

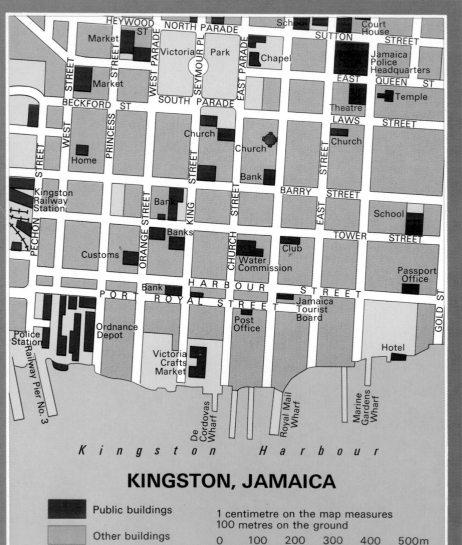

KINGSTON, JAMAICA

■ Public buildings

▨ Other buildings

☐ Parks and open spaces

1 centimetre on the map measures 100 metres on the ground

0   100   200   300   400   500m

0   1   2   3   4   5 cm

1 centimetre on the map measures
100 kilometres on the ground

0   100   200   300   400   500 km

0   1   2   3   4   5 cm

ATLANTIC

OCEAN

Tropic of Cancer

Glasgow   Edinburgh

Newcastle   Sunderland

Belfast   Middlesbrough

Leeds   Hull

Dublin   Liverpool   Manchester
Sheffield

Stoke   Nottingham

Birmingham   Coventry
ENGLAND

WALES   Luton

Cardiff   Bristol   London

Southampton

Isle of Wight

At the same scale

Grassland

Forest and woodland

Farmland

Industrial land
with many people

■ Very large town
(more than one million people)

● Large town
(less than one million people)

— International boundary

Acklin's I.

Turks and Caicos Islands
(U.K.)

Great Inagua I.

DOMINICAN
REPUBLIC

HAITI   Santiago

HISPANIOLA

Port-au-
Prince.   Santo
Domingo

Bayamon   San Juan
Carolina

Ponce

PUERTO
RICO (U.S.A.)

Virgin Is.
(U.S.A.)

Virgin Is.
(U.K.)

ST. KITTS-
NEVIS   ANTIGUA

I   N   D   I   E   S

Guadeloupe
(Fr.)

DOMINICA

BEAN   SEA

Martinique
(Fr.)

ST.
LUCIA

BARBADOS

ST. VINCENT AND
THE GRENADINES

GRENADA

Curaçao
(Neth.)

Willemstad

TOBAGO

Santa
Marta   Punto Fijo

Margarita I.   Port of
Spain

quilla   Ciénaga

Maracaibo   Cabimas

Valledupar

Maracay
Valencia

Caracas

TRINIDAD

Barcelona

Maturín

Barquisimeto

V   E   N   E   Z   U   E   L   A

Orinoco   Ciudad
Guyana

Cúcuta   San Cristóbal

Ciudad
Bolívar

OMBIA

Apure

Bucaramanga

Georgetown

© Collins ◆ Longman Atlases

Pakistan, India, Bangladesh and Sri Lanka

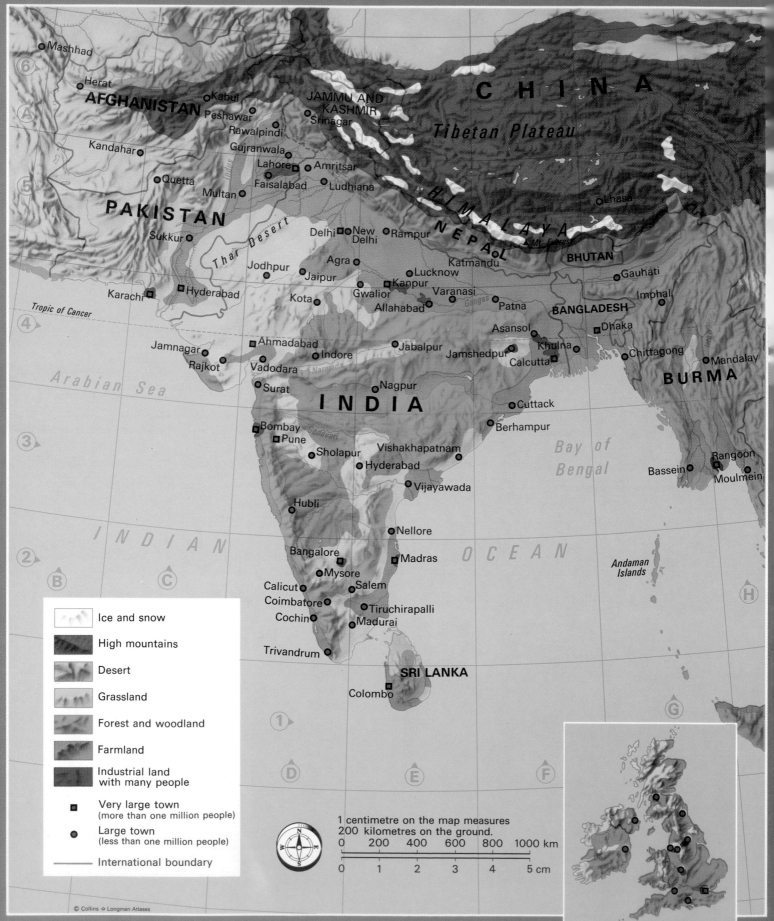

Mashhad

Herat
AFGHANISTAN
Kabul
Peshawar
Rawalpindi
Kandahar
Gujranwala
Lahore
Amritsar
Quetta
Faisalabad
Ludhiana
Multan
PAKISTAN
Sukkur
Thar Desert

JAMMU AND KASHMIR
Srinagar

CHINA
Tibetan Plateau

HIMALAYA
NEPAL
Lhasa
BHUTAN

Delhi
New Delhi
Rampur
Katmandu
Gauhati
Agra
Lucknow
Imphal
Jodhpur
Jaipur
Kanpur
Gwalior
Varanasi
Patna
BANGLADESH
Kota
Allahabad
Asansol
Dhaka
Jamnagar
Ahmadabad
Jabalpur
Khulna
Chittagong
Rajkot
Indore
Jamshedpur
Calcutta
Mandalay
Vadodara
Narmada
Surat
Nagpur
INDIA
BURMA
Karachi
Hyderabad

Tropic of Cancer

Arabian Sea

Cuttack
Bombay
Godavari
Berhampur
Pune
Bay of Bengal
Sholapur
Vishakhapatnam
Rangoon
Hyderabad
Bassein
Vijayawada
Moulmein
Hubli

INDIAN
Nellore
OCEAN
Bangalore
Madras
Andaman Islands
Mysore
Calicut
Salem
Coimbatore
Tiruchirapalli
Cochin
Madurai
Trivandrum

SRI LANKA
Colombo

Legend

Ice and snow

High mountains

Desert

Grassland

Forest and woodland

Farmland

Industrial land with many people

■ Very large town (more than one million people)

● Large town (less than one million people)

— International boundary

1 centimetre on the map measures 200 kilometres on the ground.

0   200   400   600   800   1000 km

0   1   2   3   4   5 cm

At the same scale

© Collins · Longman Atlases

56

Pakistan, India, Bangladesh and Sri Lanka are four countries in southern Asia. Compare their size with the inset map of the British Isles. Bangladesh has a larger area than England, and Pakistan is almost three times bigger than the British Isles. This map is drawn at the same scale as the map of Europe on page 35. You can see that travelling the length of India is the same as travelling the length of Europe. The maps of the Ganges Delta and the city of Calcutta show these areas in even more detail. The map of the Ganges Delta is at the same scale as the British Isles maps on pages 24 to 27. Find a map earlier in the book which is at the same scale as the map of Calcutta.

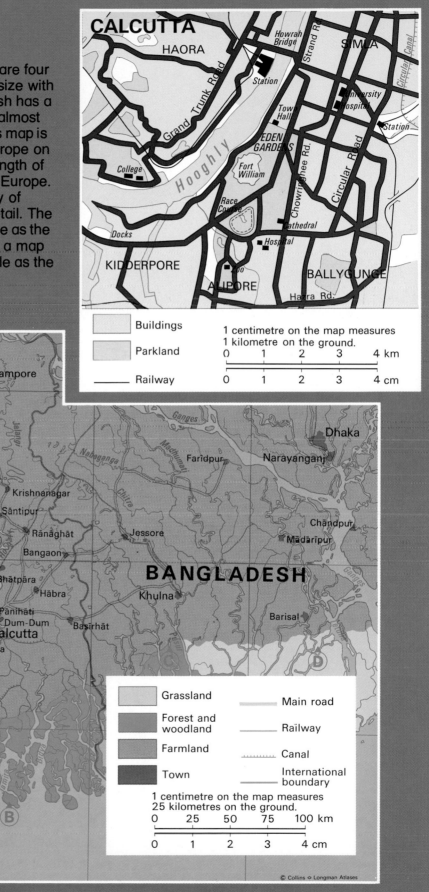

CALCUTTA

	Buildings
	Parkland
——	Railway

1 centimetre on the map measures
1 kilometre on the ground.

0   1   2   3   4 km

0   1   2   3   4 cm

THE GANGES DELTA

	Grassland	≡≡≡	Main road
	Forest and woodland	——	Railway
	Farmland	········	Canal
	Town	——	International boundary

1 centimetre on the map measures
25 kilometres on the ground.

0   25   50   75   100 km

0   1   2   3   4 cm

© Collins ◇ Longman Atlases

How a map is made

The maps you have explored in this book are the result of many people's work. The photographs on this page show the stages in the preparation and production of one type of map, from the taking of the vertical aerial photo to the printed map.

? 1 How many stages in map production are shown here?
   2 Turn to pages 46 and 47.
     List the stages needed to produce the map of Africa from the satellite photo.
   3 Why does so much work need to be done to produce an accurate map?

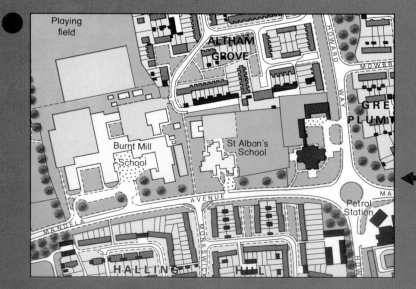

Drawing the map from the vertical aerial photo.

Checking the detail on the map on the ground.

Preparing the final map for printing.

Printing the map.

British Isles   Index

A map index helps you to find where places are on the map. On this page and on page 60 is the index for the maps of the British Isles. On pages 61, 62 and 63 is the index for the maps of the rest of the World.

The colour-coding in the index will tell you whether the feature is water (blue), land (red), or man-made (black).

A grid has been drawn over each of the maps of the British Isles on pages 24 to 27. Part of one map is shown in **A**. Each grid line on the map has been given a number.

Here is part of the index:

> **Coleraine** *town* 27 **128** 142
> **Colwyn Bay** *town* 25 **127** 147
> **Corby** *town* 25 **147** 138

If you are not sure how to use a six-figure grid reference, read pages 4 and 15 which explain how to use four- and six-figure grid references.

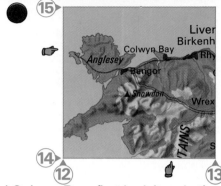

To find Colwyn Bay, first look it up in the alphabetical index. The index shows it is on the map on page 25. Next to the page number is its six-figure grid reference. This is **127 147**. Now turn to the correct page and use this grid reference to find Colwyn Bay on the map, as in **A**.

Aberdeen *town* 26 **138** 188
Aberystwyth *town* 25 **124** 137
Achill Island 27 **105** 129
Airdrie *town* 26 **126** 174
Aldershot *town* 25 **147** 124
Anglesey *island* 25 **121** 146
Aran Island 27 **107** 119
Arran *island* 26 **118** 171
Athlone *town* 27 **120** 123
Avon *river* 25 **139** 134

Ballymena *town* 27 **131** 139
Bangor *town* 25 **124** 146
Bangor *town* 27 **135** 137
Bann *river* 27 **128** 142
Bantry Bay 27 **106** 102
Barnsley *town* 25 **142** 149
Barnstaple *town* 25 **124** 122
Barrow *river* 27 **127** 115
Barrow-in-Furness *town* 24 **131** 156
Barry *town* 25 **129** 126
Basildon *town* 25 **156** 128
Basingstoke *town* 25 **144** 124
Bath *town* 25 **136** 125
Bedford *town* 25 **149** 134
Belfast *town* 27 **133** 136
Ben Nevis *mountain* 26 **121** 184
Berwick-upon-Tweed *town* 26 **139** 173
Birkenhead *town* 25 **131** 148
Birmingham *town* 25 **139** 138
Blackburn *town* 24 **135** 152
Blackpool *town* 24 **131** 152
Blackwater *river* 27 **118** 108
Boggeragh Mountains 27 **114** 108
Bognor Regis *town* 25 **148** 119
Bog of Allan 27 **125** 121
Bolton *town* 25 **135** 149
Boston *town* 25 **152** 143
Bournemouth *town* 25 **139** 118
Boyne *river* 27 **129** 125
Bradford *town* 24 **139** 152
Brighton *town* 25 **151** 119
Bristol *town* 25 **135** 126
Bristol Channel *sea* 25 **128** 124
Burnley *town* 24 **136** 152
Burton upon Trent *town* 25 **140** 141

Cambrian Mountains 25 **126** 132
Cambridge *town* 25 **153** 135
Cardiff *town* 25 **130** 127

Cardigan Bay 25 **121** 138
Carlisle *town* 24 **132** 164
Carlow *town* 27 **127** 117
Carrauntoohil *mountain* 27 **107** 107
Channel Islands 25 **134** 103
Chelmsford *town* 25 **155** 130
Cheltenham *town* 25 **138** 131
Chester *town* 25 **132** 145
Cheviot Hills 26 **135** 168
Chiltern Hills 25 **145** 127
Clew Bay 27 **108** 128
Clyde *river* 26 **127** 173
Colchester *town* 25 **158** 132
Coleraine *town* 27 **128** 142
Colwyn Bay *town* 25 **127** 147
Corby *town* 25 **147** 138
Cork *town* 27 **117** 106
Cotswold Hills 25 **136** 127
Coventry *town* 25 **141** 137
Crawley *town* 25 **151** 123
Crewe *town* 25 **135** 144

Darlington *town* 24 **141** 160
Dartmoor 25 **124** 117
Dee *river* 25 **129** 143
Dee *river* 26 **136** 188
Derby *town* 25 **142** 142
Dingle Bay 27 **104** 108
Don *river* 26 **134** 189
Doncaster *town* 25 **144** 149
Donegal Bay 27 **115** 135
Douglas *town* 24 **122** 156
Drogheda *town* 27 **131** 126
Dublin *town* 27 **131** 128
Dumfries *town* 26 **129** 166
Dundalk Bay 27 **131** 129
Dundee *town* 26 **132** 181
Dunfermline *town* 26 **130** 177
Durham *town* 24 **141** 163

Eastbourne *town* 25 **154** 119
Edinburgh *town* 26 **131** 175
Elgin *town* 26 **130** 194
Ellesmere Port *town* 25 **132** 146
England *country* 25 **139** 144
English Channel *sea* 25 **133** 111
Ennis *town* 27 **113** 117
Erne *river* 27 **123** 133
Exeter *town* 25 **128** 118
Exmoor 25 **126** 123

Falkirk *town* 26 **127** 176
Falmouth *town* 25 **116** 112
Firth of Clyde 26 **120** 171
Firth of Lorn 26 **113** 178
Folkestone *town* 25 **161** 123
Forth *river* 26 **125** 172
Fort William *town* 26 **119** 185

Galty Mountains 27 **117** 111
Galway *town* 27 **113** 122
Gillingham *town* 25 **156** 126
Glasgow *town* 26 **124** 174
Gloucester *town* 25 **136** 131
Grampian Mountains 26 **122** 182
Greenock *town* 26 **122** 175
Grimsby *town* 25 **151** 150
Guernsey *island* 25 **132** 105

Hamilton *town* 26 **126** 173
Harlow *town* 25 **153** 130
Harris *island* 26 **108** 196
Harrogate *town* 24 **142** 154
Hartlepool *town* 24 **143** 162
Hastings *town* 25 **157** 120
Hawick *town* 26 **134** 169
Hebrides *islands* 26 **109** 181
Hereford *town* 25 **133** 133
Huddersfield *town* 25 **140** 150
Hull *town* 24 **149** 152
Humber *river* 24 **148** 152

Inverness *town* 26 **125** 192
Ipswich *town* 25 **160** 133
Irish Sea 27 **137** 127
Islay *island* 26 **112** 174
Isle of Man 24 **122** 158
Isle of Wight 25 **145** 117
Isles of Scilly 25 **107** 111

Jersey *island* 25 **138** 102
Jura *island* 26 **114** 175

Kidderminster *town* 25 **137** 136
Kilkenny *town* 27 **125** 114
Killarney *town* 27 **109** 108
Kilmarnock *town* 26 **123** 171
Kirkcaldy *town* 26 **131** 177
Kirkwall *town* 26 **132** 209

Index

Rest of the World   Index

A grid has been drawn over each of the maps of the rest of the World. Part of one map is shown in **B**. On these maps each column has been given a letter, and each row a number.

Here is part of the index:

> **Sverdlovsk** *town* 48 **E7**
> **Swaziland** *country* 47 **F2**
> **Sweden** *country* 36 **H4**

The letter–number grid references name each grid square. The letter names each column, the number each row. The grid reference names the grid square where the lettered column and the numbered row meet.

To find Swaziland, first look it up in the alphabetical index. The index shows it is on the map on page 47. Next to the page number is its letter–number grid reference. This is **F2**. Now turn to the correct page and use the grid reference to find Swaziland on the map, as in **B**.

Abidjan *town* 47 **B5**
Accra *town* 47 **B5**
Addis Ababa *town* 47 **F5**
Adelaide *town* 52 **D2**
Afghanistan *country* 48 **E5**
Ahmadabad *town* 56 **D4**
Albania *country* 39 **F3**
Alexandria *town* 47 **E8**
Algeria *country* 47 **B7**
Algiers *town* 47 **C8**
Alice Springs *town* 52 **D3**
Amazon *river* 51 **E6**
Amritsar *town* 56 **D5**
Amsterdam *town* 36 **F2**
Anchorage *town* 50 **B7**
Andes *mountains* 51 **C2**
Andorra *country* 38 **C3**
Andropov *town* 37 **M3**
Angola *country* 47 **D3**
Ankara *town* 48 **B6**
Annaba *town* 47 **C8**
Antananarivo *town* 47 **G3**
Antarctica *region* 53
Antigua *country* 55 **E3**
Antofagasta *town* 51 **C4**
Antwerp *town* 38 **D5**
Arabian Sea 56 **B4**
Aracaju *town* 51 **G5**
Araguaia *river* 51 **E6**
Aral Sea 48 **D6**
Arctic Ocean *sea* 53
Arequipa *town* 51 **C5**
Argentina *country* 51 **D2**
Århus *town* 36 **H3**
Arkansas *river* 50 **F4**
Armavir *town* 39 **K3**
Asansol *town* 56 **F4**
Asmara *town* 47 **F6**
Aswan *town* 47 **F7**
Athens *town* 39 **G2**
Atlanta *town* 50 **H4**
Atlantic Ocean *sea* 51 **E8**
Auckland *town* 52 **H2**
Australia *country* 52 **C3**
Austria *country* 38 **E4**

Baffin Bay 50 **J8**
Baffin Island 50 **H8**
Baghdad *town* 48 **C5**
Bahamas *country* 54 **B5**
Bahrain *country* 48 **D4**
Baku *town* 48 **C6**
Baltic Sea 36 **I3**
Baltimore *town* 50 **I4**

Bamako *town* 47 **B6**
Bandung *town* 48 **I1**
Bangalore *town* 56 **D2**
Bangkok *town* 48 **I3**
Bangladesh *country* 56 **F4**
Bangui *town* 47 **D5**
Barbados *country* 55 **F2**
Barcelona *town* 38 **C3**
Barquisimeto *town* 55 **D2**
Barranquilla *town* 51 **C8**
Basel *town* 38 **D4**
Bastia *town* 38 **E3**
Bayamon *town* 55 **D3**
Bay of Bengal 56 **F3**
Bay of Biscay 38 **B4**
Beijing *town* 48 **J5**
Belém *town* 51 **F6**
Belgium *country* 38 **C5**
Belgrade *town* 39 **G3**
Belize *country* 50 **H2**
Belo Horizonte *town* 51 **F5**
Benghazi *town* 47 **E8**
Benin *country* 47 **C5**
Bergen *town* 36 **G4**
Berhampur *town* 56 **F3**
Berlin *town* 36 **H2**
Berne *town* 38 **D4**
Bhutan *country* 56 **F5**
Bilbao *town* 38 **B3**
Black Sea 39 **I3**
Blantyre *town* 47 **F3**
Bogotá *town* 51 **C7**
Bolivia *country* 51 **D5**
Bologna *town* 38 **E3**
Bombay *town* 56 **D3**
Bonn *town* 38 **D5**
Bordeaux *town* 38 **C3**
Borneo *island* 48 **J2**
Boston *town* 50 **I5**
Botswana *country* 47 **E2**
Bouaké *town* 47 **B5**
Brasília *town* 51 **F5**
Braşov *town* 39 **H4**
Bratislava *town* 39 **F4**
Brazil *country* 51 **D6**
Brazzaville *town* 47 **D4**
Bremen *town* 36 **G2**
Brisbane *town* 52 **F3**
Brunei *country* 48 **J2**
Brussels *town* 38 **D5**
Bryansk *town* 37 **L2**
Bucaramanga *town* 51 **C7**
Bucharest *town* 39 **H3**
Budapest *town* 39 **F4**

Buenos Aires *town* 51 **E3**
Bulawayo *town* 47 **E2**
Bulgaria *country* 39 **G3**
Burkina Faso *country* 47 **B6**
Burma *country* 48 **H4**
Burundi *country* 47 **F4**

Cabimas *town* 55 **C2**
Cádiz *town* 38 **A2**
Cairo *town* 47 **F7**
Calais *town* 38 **C5**
Calcutta *town* 57 **B2**
Callao *town* 51 **C5**
Camagüey *town* 54 **B4**
Cameroon *country* 47 **C5**
Campinas *town* 51 **F4**
Campos *town* 51 **F4**
Canada *country* 50 **E6**
Canary Islands 47 **A7**
Canberra *town* 52 **E2**
Cape Town 47 **D1**
Caracas *town* 51 **D8**
Caribbean Sea 54 **B3**
Carolina *town* 55 **D3**
Carpathians *mountains* 39 **G4**
Cartagena *town* 51 **C7**
Casablanca *town* 47 **B8**
Caspian Sea 48 **D5**
Caucasus *mountains* 48 **C6**
Central African Republic
  country 47 **D5**
Chad *country* 47 **D6**
Chang Jiang *river* 48 **I5**
Cheboksary *town* 37 **O3**
Chelyabinsk *town* 48 **E7**
Chengdu *town* 48 **I5**
Cherepovets *town* 37 **M3**
Chernigov *town* 37 **L2**
Chernovtsy *town* 39 **H4**
Chicago *town* 50 **H5**
Chile *country* 51 **C4**
China *country* 48 **H5**
Christchurch *town* 52 **H1**
Churchill *town* 50 **G6**
Ciénaga *town* 55 **C2**
Cincinnati *town* 50 **H4**
Ciudad Guyana *town* 55 **E1**
Clermont Ferrand *town* 38 **C4**
Cologne *town* 38 **D5**
Colombia *country* 51 **C7**
Colombo *town* 56 **E1**
Colorado *river* 50 **E4**
Conakry *town* 47 **A5**
Congo *country* 47 **D4**

Constanţa *town* 39 **H3**
Constantine *town* 47 **C8**
Copenhagen *town* 36 **H3**
Cordoba *town* 38 **B2**
Córdoba *town* 51 **D3**
Corsica *island* 38 **D3**
Costa Rica *country* 50 **H1**
Cracow *town* 39 **G4**
Craiova *town* 39 **G3**
Crete *island* 39 **G2**
Cuba *country* 54 **B4**
Cubango *river* 47 **D3**
Curitiba *town* 51 **F4**
Cuttack *town* 56 **F4**
Cyprus *country* 48 **A5**
Czechoslovakia *country* 39 **F5**

Dakar *town* 47 **A6**
Dallas *town* 50 **G4**
Damascus *town* 48 **B5**
Danube *river* 39 **H3**
Dar es Salaam *town* 47 **F4**
Darling *river* 52 **E2**
Darwin *town* 52 **D4**
Debrecen *town* 39 **G4**
Delhi *town* 56 **D5**
Denmark *country* 36 **G3**
Denver *town* 50 **F4**
Detroit *town* 50 **H5**
Dhaka *town* 57 **D3**
Dijon *town* 38 **D4**
Djibouti *country* 47 **G6**
Dneprodzerzhinsk *town* 39 **J4**
Dnepropetrovsk *town* 39 **J4**
Dnestr *river* 39 **H4**
Dnieper *river* 39 **I4**
Dominica *country* 55 **E3**
Dominican Republic *country*
  55 **D3**
Donets *river* 39 **K4**
Dordogne *river* 38 **C4**
Dortmund *town* 38 **D5**
Douala *town* 47 **C5**
Dresden *town* 36 **H2**
Dubai *town* 48 **D4**
Dunedin *town* 52 **H1**
Durban *town* 47 **F2**
Düsseldorf *town* 38 **D5**
Dzherzhinsk *town* 37 **N3**

East Germany *country* 36 **H2**
Ebro *river* 38 **B3**
Ecuador *country* 51 **B6**
Edmonton *town* 50 **E6**

Index

Index

Teacher's notes

MAP WORK SECTION

	Ideas / Skills	Resources	Extension activities
2–3	● relating ground level, oblique and vertical photos with map ● use of key and map symbols ● using written information on the map ● describing routes and what can be seen	● oblique/vertical photos of school area ● photos of features in school locality ● large scale OS map of area around school ● photos/large scale maps of other areas	● use OS map and walk round school area locating features, noting how shown on map; update map ● make a model of area around school ● devise shortest routes from school to local features
4	● finding and giving grid references ● introduction to 4-figure grid references ● 4-figure grid references names grid square NE of intersection of lines ● use of a smaller scale map	● use of school area map with grid overlay to practise grid references ● grid sheets with numbers marked along bottom and side, and unnumbered	● on grid sheets, children mark list of grid references, then join them up to produce a shape; to devise their own shape, list grid references, ask another to draw shape from grid reference list ● play battleships
5	● use of 4/8 compass points ● reinforce idea of symbols and need for key ● use of smaller scale map; OS 1:10 000	● OS maps of local area including 1:10 000 ● direction compasses: large for demonstration, small for personal use	● give and follow compass directions walking round playground/school ● orient local map to area using compass ● give and follow compass directions on map
6–7	● idea of features drawn to scale ● introduction to measuring distances on map; use of scale bar ● a distance on the map represents a distance on the real ground ● plans and maps can be drawn to different scales; larger area shown, smaller the scale	● plans of objects in room, room plans, school plans all drawn to scale, OS large scale maps of area ● different sizes of squared paper from 1mm to 4cm ● metre/centimetre rulers, tape measures, trundle wheel	● measure lengths and distances on plans/maps, using scale bar ● make cm scale bar on a strip of paper to go with each map, so that it can be laid on map ● draw scale plans of features in room and of room/school building/grounds – draw on squared paper, discuss appropriate scale
8–9	● use of map to show that changes have happened, and can be planned for/to an area ● comparing maps/photos of the same area from different dates ● maps become dated ● ideas of change and continuity	● old and current large scale OS maps of school area; any other old maps of school area ● old and current photos of area around school ● overhead projector (OHP) transparencies of old and current maps	● go out round area of school using an old map to find way around, note changes ● use old map to make a model of how area used to look; plan how area could develop ● on OHP lay transparency of current map over old map to see where change has occurred
10–11	● variety of maps we see, use, and get information from ● way different maps show features	● maps of different sorts from papers, brochures, books, signs, postcards, games, posters, magazines, computer software	● collect a range of maps; compare for purpose, content, style, usefulness, clarity, accuracy ● design maps for specific purposes
12	● oblique view of a hilly landscape	● photos and pictures of hilly landscapes	● identify features both natural and man-made
13	● cartographers have used different ways to show hills and slopes on maps: hillocks, hachures, hill-shading ● ideas of shape, slope, location on map	● old maps showing hilly landscapes locally and elsewhere ● large scale map of area around school, local street map	● discuss changes in way landshape shown on maps ● use on local street map, work out way of showing slope of ground: where, how much, direction ● make, then map model of an undulating landscape
14–15	● spot height as symbol to show height ● contour as symbol to show shape, slope of land ● practice using contours at 5m intervals on OS 1:10 000 and 1:25 000 scale maps ● introduction to 6-figure grid reference ● reinforcement of use of symbols and key	● OS 1:10 000 and 1:25 000 scale map of local and other areas, showing contours and grids ● photos/drawings of slopes/hills, and contour maps to match, showing shape ● photos of slopes in local and other areas	● use OS map and walk area where contour lines show slope; discuss before and on site how contour lines show slope of ground ● from map describe walk on a route, saying whether going up/down hill, steep/gentle ● on map find areas shown in photos
16–19	● greater generalisation of symbol as scale reduced; greater need for key ● need to select what is included in map as scale reduces ● comparison of maps of different scales ● reinforce use of map skills on different scales of maps	● variety of OS and other maps of local areas at range of scales ● centimetre ruler ● pipecleaners/thin wire/cotton/string lengths to help measure crooked distances on maps	● examine pair of maps of different scales to see how same area is shown; discuss way each map shows what it does ● measure 'crooked' distances on maps: lay cotton/wire along road, bending to its shape; when length marked, straighten and lay along scale bar to measure distance
20–21	● use of margin information about maps ● idea of a thematic map ● maps show only a selection of information	● OHP maps of an area each showing different thematic information ● maps that show specific themes clearly	● lay several transparencies over each other; discuss problem of reading any one clearly; show individually ● develop checklist of points for a useful map